THE LITERARY BIBLE
OF THOMAS JEFFERSON

THE

LITERARY BIBLE

OF

THOMAS JEFFERSON

HIS COMMONPLACE BOOK

OF PHILOSOPHERS AND POETS

with an introduction

by

GILBERT CHINARD

Professor in The Johns Hopkins University

GREENWOOD PRESS, PUBLISHERS
NEW YORK

Originally published in 1928 by, and reprinted
with the permission of, The Johns Hopkins Press

First Greenwood Reprinting 1969

Library of Congress Catalogue Card Number 73-90537

SBN 8371-2251-1

PRINTED IN UNITED STATES OF AMERICA

INTRODUCTION

Jefferson remains to this day if not the greatest figure of the American Revolution, perhaps the most elusive and most fascinating. His interests were so varied and his life so full, that historians do not seem to have been able to draw his portrait with the bold strokes and vivid touches which appeal to popular imagination. And yet under his apparent versatility and in spite of his alleged cosmopolitanism he was probably more truly and more fundamentally a representative American than any of his contemporaries. Among the men of his generation, he was the first, and almost the only one to combine the refinements of classical and European cultures with the sturdy qualities of the pioneer. He had very early the vision of a greater America which would outgrow the thirteen original states, and he lived to work toward the fulfilment of his dream. But he was too intensely American to wish to modify the natural characteristics of his country and impose upon it the veneer of any foreign civilisation. For all his faith in the people and their ultimate possibilities and achievements he had no love for what he called " the rabble ". His early education made him an aristocrat, and an aristocrat of the intellect he remained to the end of his days. He developed very early certain traits, tendencies and inclinations which are perfectly recognizable throughout his life and became more pronounced as he grew older.

GILBERT CHINARD   I

The recently published *Commonplace Book* of
Thomas Jefferson (1) contains ample evidence of the
breadth of his information on legal and political
subjects. It is of little help however in ascertaining
the literary tastes of the most widely read American
of his generation. The catalogue of his library,
written in his own hand and preserved in the Cool-
idge Collections of the Massachusetts Historical
Society, is so extensive as to be practically useless.
One sees clearly from it that Jefferson undertook to
collect a library of the best books in every branch
of human knowledge. But even admitting that he
may have glanced through most of these many volumes, neither he, nor any one, could have read them
from cover to cover, and at any rate we are left without
any precise indication in regard to Jefferson's literary
preferences and favorite authors.

The allusions scattered in his letters, the lists of
books he drew up on several occasions for some of
his friends, are somewhat more conclusive. But
these lists themselves were made for a particular
object, to suit the needs of a particular person and
are far from satisfactory. It is known in a general
way that Jefferson was a fervent admirer of the classics,
that he was a very good scholar, that he had a good
knowledge of French and Italian literatures, and had
studied with much interest the technique of English
poetry. His correspondence, to be sure, contains
abundant information on his political views, but
comparatively little on his personal affairs and
preoccupations. It does not seem that Jefferson ever
kept a diary in which he committed to paper the qualms
and dreams that filled his mind when, as a young
man is wont to do, he examined the problem of the

(1) *The Commonplace Book of Thomas Jefferson. A Repertory of his
Ideas on Government. With an introduction by* Gilbert Chinard. The Johns
Hopkins Press, 1926.

universe. The only precise knowledge of the earlier period of his life we can gather is contained in a very few letters to his friend Peter Carr, and in the first page of the *Autobiography* drawn up when he was seventy-seven. And yet to know a man, it is essential not only to see him act or hear him talk, but also to have access into that " secret garden " where he takes refuge from the world. With characteristic diffidence, except perhaps for the last fifteen years of his life, Jefferson jealously guarded all access to this " garden ". But what he did not express himself he copied from the philosophers and poets who were the friends and mentors of his school days.

The fact that the literary *Commonplace Book* we are publishing here for the first time was until a recent date kept in private hands, can alone explain why historians and biographers of Jefferson have not heretofore made use of it. Were it only a collection of the most beautiful passages of famous writers, such an anthology, since compiled by Jefferson, would be worthy of publication. It is something more however. This worn little volume, these closely written and now faded pages give us an opportunity to penetrate the real personality of Jefferson. If, as we believe and hope to show, this much thumbed little book was compiled by Jefferson during his student days, it could rightly be called : " Jefferson self-revealed ". For it contains the maxims and principles which so impressed his still plastic mind, that by them he was to govern the rest of his life.

A curious passage, found under March 1770 in one of his unpublished memorandum books, may well serve to illustrate this point. Jefferson was then a very active law practitioner, he was building a house, and was keeping tab on his slaves and laborers. Most of the entries consist of fees received, of cases tried and of technical recipes. But once, after noting carefully that " 4 good fellows, a lad and 2 girls of about 16 each, have dug in my cellar a place in 8 hrs 1/2, 3 feet deep, 8 feet wide and 16 1/2 feet long ", he stopped to recapitulate the most striking mottos, definitions and maxims he had gathered in his readings.   Here are some of the most significant : μετρὸν δ'ἐπὶ πᾶσιν ἄριστον — no liberty no life — ἀνέχου καὶ ἀπέχου — *bonum quod honestum* — *macte virtute esto* — οἰστέον καὶ ἐλπίστεον — *nil desperandum* — *faber suae quisque fortunæ* — *un dieu un roy* — *fari quae sentiat* — what is is right — *ex recto decus* — οὐδεὶς οὐδάμου — *ne cede malis sed contra audentior ito* — Long life, long health, long pleasure and a friend (Pope) — The sleepy eye that speaks to the melting soul (Pope) — *Non votum nobis sed patria. — Fiat justitia ruat cœlum.*

Such a heterogeneous collection bears the mark of the times.   Very few of these sharply coined maxims would be found in the diary of a modern college graduate, supposing that our college graduates still keep diaries.   By such maxims, however, young men of the eighteenth century were wont to form their resolutions and to regulate their actions.   They are characteristic of the man as well as of the period.   In those remote days the study of the classics was more than a luxury or a painful task.   It was an essential part in the moral foundation of many of the men who framed the American institutions.   It contributed to give a stoic tone to their characters and a clearer ring to their utterances.   The " substantific marrow " of great authors was transmuted into their own substance ; it played in their lives a part equal if not greater than that of " the moral teachings of Jesus ".   Thus this second *Commonplace Book* is the missing complement of *Jefferson's Bible* ; it is quite as necessary for a true understanding of the personality of the man who wrote the Declaration of Independence and formulated the democratic creed of America.

In its present condition, this manuscript forms a

little book, of 119 leaves bound in worn old leather.
The handwriting shows clearly that this collection
of abstracts was undertaken by Jefferson at an early
time of his life and continued, for a period that
we shall attempt to determine, after his hand had
acquired its later well-known characteristics. On the
fly-leaf the following note was written by the
donor who presented the document to the Library
of Congress :

> This book I always understood to have been a scrap book used,
> by Thomas Jefferson before his hand was fully formed and up
> to late in life, in the end is some printed matter and a poem of
> Mrs Barbuld (Barbauld) in Mrs Randolph's handwriting. She
> always kept this book of her father's among her treasures.
>
> M. J. BURKE.
> *Alexandria*, Va. Jan. 29th, 1898.

On one point however I would beg to differ with
the donor. I do not believe that Jefferson added
" up to late in life " to his collection of abstracts,
with the possible exception of very few entries. The
paper on which he wrote is the Holland paper com-
monly used in America before the Revolution. Some
of the loose leaves which originally constituted the
manuscript were lost by Jefferson himself, as he has
written in his own hand (*wanting*) at the bottom of
several pages before giving them to the binder.

THE GREEK AUTHORS

In this *Commonplace Book*, the Greek authors are
represented by Homer, Herodotus, Euripides, Anacreon and Quintus Smyrnæus. Nine quotations
from the *Iliad*, three from the *Odyssey*, to which
must be added seventeen from Pope's translation,
attest Jefferson's fondness for the old epic. To

matters of mythology, descriptions of battles and
grandiose comparisons, Jefferson apparently paid
no attention whatever. He evidently saw in Homer
a repository of the wisdom of an ancient civilization.
From him he collected verses in which the poet
expressed his views on life and human destiny, — a
courageous, stoic and often disenchanted philosophy.
It is summed up in two lines of Pope's translation :

> To labour is the lot of man below ;
> And when Jove gave us life he gave us woe.

We are already familiar with Jefferson the statesman
and the man of politics and we know the distaste he
so often evidenced for " idle metaphysical disquisitions ". Not until he had retired to his retreat of
Monticello did he indulge in discussions on the nature
of the soul, on life and death, with a few chosen
friends such as Thomas Cooper and John Adams.
But even at that time he persistently maintained that
" the business of life " was life, he staunchly refused
to admit feeling any qualms at his approaching death
and composed himself for his eternal sleep like a sage
of the ancient days. And yet anyone who reads
between the lines or simply scrutinizes more carefully
the letters written during the Monticello period will
easily perceive, behind the Stoic mask, a certain
anxiety, and throbs of pain which the well brought
up Virginian was too proud to reveal even to his
most intimate friends. Age had brought with it
resignation and acceptance, but from the abstracts
made by Jefferson and copied in his commonplace
book it is quite evident that at an earlier period he
was deeply concerned with the riddle of death and
that most of his meditations centered around it. In
Homer he did not find an answer to the tragic enigma
since

> Death is the worst ; a Fate we all must try,

but with the help of the poet he strove to formulate
a substitute for the consoling beliefs he had already
abandoned :

> And, for our country, 'tis a Bliss to die.
> The gallant Man tho' slain in Fight he be,
> Yet leaves his Nation safe, his Children free ;
> Entails a Debt on all the gratefull State :
> His own brave Friends shall glory in his Fate ;
> His Wife live honour'd, all his Race succeed ·
> And late Posterity enjoy the deed.
>
> (*II.* 15, 582. *Pope's translation, see p.*127).

That he was familiar with the other aspects of the
poem is however quite certain. Homer he knew
well enough to put his finger upon a definite passage,
on reading in an English paper of the invention of a
new wheel :

> I see by the Journal of this morning », wrote he to Crèvecœur in
> 1787, « that they are robbing us of another of our inventions to
> give it to the English. The writer, indeed, only admits them to
> have revived what he thinks was known to the Greeks, that is, the
> making the circumference of a wheel of one single piece... The
> writer in the paper, supposes the English workman got his idea
> from Homer. But it is more likely the Jersey farmer got his idea
> from thence, because ours are the only farmers who can read
> Homer : because, too, the Jersey practice is precisely that stated
> by Homer : the English practice very different. Homer's words
> are (comparing a young hero killed by Ajax to a poplar felled by a
> workman) literally thus : " He fell on the ground, like a poplar,
> which has grown smooth, in the west part of a great meadow ;
> with its branches shooting from its summit. But the chariot
> maker, with the sharp ax, has felled it, that he may bend a wheel
> for a beautiful chariot. It lies drying on the banks of the river... "
>
> (To Monsieur de Crève Cœur, Jan. 15, 1787. *Memorial edition,*
> VI, 55).

The statement that even in those days the New
Jersey farmers could read Homer needs be taken
with a grain of salt, but what cannot be doubted is
the profound admiration and gratitude of the Virgi-

nian for the old Greek poet who had revealed to him
the beauty of the ancient world, as evidenced in a
letter written to Joseph Priestly :

I enjoy Homer in his own language infinitely beyond Pope's
translation of him, and both beyond the dull narrative of the same
event by Dares Phrygius : and it is an innocent enjoyment. I
thank on my knees Him who directed my early education, for
having put into my possession this rich source of delight : and
I would not exchange it for anything which I could then have
acquired, and have not acquired.

(To Dr. J. Priestly. Jan. 27, 1800. *M. E.* X, 146.)

That he was not unappreciative of the literary value
of his favorite author appears in another letter :

Did the Athenians consider the Doric, the Ionian, the Aeolic,
and other dialects, as disfiguring or as beautifying their language ?
Did they fastidiously disavow Herodotus, Pindar, Theocritus,
Sappho, Alcæus, or Grecian writers ? On the contrary, they
were sensible that the variety of dialects, still infinitely varied by
poetical license, constituted the riches of their language, and made
the Grecian Homer the first of poets, as he must ever remain, until
a language equally ductile and copious shall again be spoken.

(To John Waldo. August 16, 1813. *M. E.* XIII, 341).

But before all, Homer was for Jefferson a teacher
of courageous resignation, an inspirer of heroic
dreams, a master and a guide ; and he turned to him,
when after the death of his wife he tried to express his
grief. In the epitaph he wrote then for the tomb
of Martha Jefferson " torn from him by death " he
inscribed two lines from the *Iliad* :

Εἰ δὲ θανόντων περ καταλήθοντ' εἰν 'Αΐδαο,
Αὐτὰρ ἐγώ κακεῖθι φιλου μεμνήσομ' ἑταίρου.

(Iliad, XXII, 389)

If in the house of Hades men forget their dead,
Yet will I even there remember my dear companion.

From Euripides, obviously less heroic and more modern in tone, Jefferson derived a similar lesson. We possess only the abstracts he made from *Hecuba*, *Orestes*, *Phœnissæ*, *Medea* and *Hippolytus* ; but there is reason to believe that his reading of the Greek dramatist was even more extensive, for in the part listed under Euripides no fewer than eighteen pages are missing. This probably accounts for the lack of abstracts from such dramas as *Alcestis*, *Andromache* and *Iphigeneia*. He was certainly attracted by the political maxims of the Greek writer and by his pessimistic turn of mind. In him it was possible to find a stern lesson on the ingratitude of the crowd :

In this are most cities harmed whenever a man who is noble and zealous wins no higher prize than baser men (*Hecuba*, 306).

Even before he entered political life, he was warned by his Greek teacher against the ways of the demagogue who caters to the vilest instincts of the multitude :

Thankless is your kind, all you who are striving to gain the reputation of a popular speaker ; may you remain unknown to me, you who care not if you hurt your friends, provided you say something that pleases the crowd (*Hecuba*, 254).

Or again :

Alas, no one among mortals is free ; for either he is the slave of wealth or fortune, or else the populace or legal technicalities compel him to resort to practices that are contrary to his belief (*Hecuba*, 864).

Jefferson however was not unaware of the other aspects of Euripides' subtle and many sided philosophy of life. How the young lawyer whose love of liberty was kindled by Patrick Henry's fiery speeches must have approved such statements as " equality is the natural law of man " (*Phœnissæ*, 541) !

How the man who cooperated so enthusiastically in the simplification of legal procedure in Virginia must have agreed with the statement that

> Plain is the word of truth, and of elaborate interpretations justice has no need ; of herself she is fitting. But the unrighteous word, being unsound, needs cunning allurements (*Phœnissae*, 472).

But, curiously enough, most of the selections reflect the natural dispositions of a man who distrusts the masses and takes pride in his birth and in his ancestry. This is at least one of the presumptions which led us to believe that most of these abstracts were compiled rather early in the life of Jefferson, and certainly before he had formulated to himself his democratic creed. After Euripides he repeats that :

> To be of the noble born gives a peculiar distinction clearly marked among men, and the noble name increases in lustre in those who are worthy (*Hecuba*, 379).

or again that :

> Strange if bad soil, obtaining good season from Providence, bears a rich harvest, while good soil, lacking what it must have, gives evil fruit. Among men he who is evil is ever aught but base, and the noble man is noble, neither through circumstance does he mar his nature, but is ever upright (*Hecuba*, 592).

At that time at least Jefferson was not the fierce enemy of aristocracies that later he was represented to be.

Lovers of Euripides may be disappointed at not finding among these abstracts some of the most famous passages of the Greek poet. These omissions are particularly striking in the case of Orestes, the most deeply human of Euripidean dramas, and yet out of so many unforgettable lines Jefferson quoted only the beginning of the invocation to sleep :

> O sovereign oblivion of suffering, how wise thou art and to the unhappy a god to be invoked with prayers (*Orestes*, 213).

Whether he felt the charm and human tenderness of the drama can only be surmised ; but all in all, he copied only those passages which contained a moral teaching and from which he could draw a lesson. Very few of the thoughts thus collected could not be found expressed almost in the same words in his correspondence. There are few indeed that did not echo persistently in his memory and could not serve as an illustration to some episode of his life. The Euripides found in the *Commonplace Book* may not be the true Euripides but this was Jefferson's Euripides, a treasure of experience and of disenchanted and yet courageous wisdom.

Of the other Greek authors quoted here much less needs be said. From Herodotus he collected three passages of mere historical interest ; from Anacreon two stanzas on the brevity of life and a similar passage from Quintus Smyrnæus. Whatever may have been his enjoyment of Greek poetry there is little doubt, from the evidence available in the *Commonplace Book*, that Jefferson read the Greek classics for their practical value and in order to derive from them a moral profit. But his knowledge of Greek literature was more than a superficial one that would have enabled him to shine in learned society, and to make literary allusions in his correspondence. Through constant and systematic study he really lived in the commerce of the Greeks. From them he took only what he could assimilate and put to use. He seems to have neglected the tragic grandeur of Æschylus, the subtle and pervasive irony of Lucian and he cared even less for Plato. There is no proof that he read the latter in his youth and the only mention he ever made of him shows how far he was from the Greek philosopher :

I amused myself with reading seriously Plato's Republic. I am wrong, however, in calling it amusement, for it was the heaviest task-work I ever went through. I had occasionally before taken

up some of his other works, but scarcely ever had patience to go
through a whole dialogue.   While reading through the whimsies,
the puerilities and unintelligible jargon of this work, I laid it down
often to ask myself how it could have been, that the world should
have consented to give reputation to such nonsense as this ?   How
the *soi-disant* Christian world, indeed, should have done it, it is a
piece of historical curiosity.   But how could the Roman good
sense do it ?   And particularly, how could Cicero bestow such
eulogies on Plato ?   Although Cicero did not wield the dense
logic of Demosthenes yet he was able, learned, laborious, practised
in the business of the world, and honest.   He could not be the
dupe of mere style, of which he was himself the first master in the
world.

(To John Adams, July 5, 1814. *M. E.* XIV, 148).

Such a scorn for mere speculations he evidenced
all his life.   But at a time when his Christian faith
was shaken and he may have felt the danger of falling
into agnosticism, he sought and found in the old
Greek poets a solid foundation on which to build
his moral creed.   From them he learned the lesson
of experience : not to trust blindly the uneducated
crowd and not to expect too much from life ; not to
dream of a chimerical bliss, for the lot of the average
man is a unhappy one, but to do his duty, without
expecting to be rewarded by public gratitude, to
cultivate his friends and love his country even to the
point of self sacrifice.   To what extent he remained
faithful to this stern and heroic program is a point for
his biographers to determine.   It will suffice here
to indicate what part it played in his moral formation
and in the shaping of his ideals.

THE LATIN AUTHORS

Among the Latin poets, Virgil is represented by
but few quotations, none of them of particular signi-
ficance ; — Ovid by four, in which the same accep-

tance of the inevitable we have already noted is
advocated :

One must easily bear whatever one deserves, but undeserved
punishment brings with it grief. (*Heroids, Œnon to Paris*, V, 7).

and

Whatever may happen will be better than what is now. (*Heroids, Sappho to Phaon*, v. 177).

To Horace Jefferson granted more space, in all
twelve quotations, among which are some passages
familiar to every school boy : " The snows have fled ;
already the grass is returning to the fields... ; Pale
Death knocks equally at the door of the poor man's
cabin and at the palaces of the rulers... ; Enjoy to-
day and put as little trust as possible in the morrow...;
O country when shall I see thee again ".

More characteristic of the time and of Jefferson
himself is probably the passage beginning " *Absentem
qui rodit amicum... hic niger est : hunc tu Romane caveto*,
He who tears to pieces a friend behind his back...
that man has a dark soul. Keep away from him,
O Roman ". The place occupied by friendship in
the literature and in the sentimental life of the eighteenth century, as it has often been observed, is probably greater than the place occupied by love. In
that respect Jefferson followed the tendency of his
time. It is particularly apparent in several of his
selections from Homer and Euripides. With the
characteristic restraint of the gentleman, he forbore
to give expression to that sentiment in his correspondence, but that he esteemed friends beyond all treasure is well known, and in the midst of political
strife the lines he had copied from Euripides must
more than once have come back to his memory :

Nothing is better than a reliable friend, not riches, not absolute
sovereignty. Nay more, the crowd is not to be reckoned with, in
exchange for a noble friend. (*Orestes*, v. 1155).

Livy is quoted only once and so are Statius and Manilius, the latter appearing quite at the end of the manuscript in a quotation evidently added long after the main body of the *Commonplace Book* was compiled. Seneca is represented by two quotations from *Medea* and Catullus by one. Here the number of quotations cannot serve as an index to the degree of familiarity of Jefferson with these authors.

The most significant of the Latin abstracts are by far those from Cicero. Curiously enough, Jefferson did not share the traditional and almost universal admiration for his oratory. Not a real orator himself, writing in a simple and direct style, he had very little use for the well rounded periods of the Roman orator. In a letter to John Wayles Eppes he deplored the " ill effects " of the long speeches that were the fashion in the House of Representatives and even made Cicero responsible for that evil :

The models for that oratory which is to produce the greatest effect by securing the attention of hearers and readers, are to be found in Livy, Tacitus, Sallust, and most assuredly not in Cicero. I doubt if there is a man in the world who can now read one of his orations through but as a peice of task-work. (To John Wayles Eppes. January 17, 1810. *M. E.* XII, 343).

If only this sensible advice had been followed we would have been spared some of the oratorical monstruosities of parliamentary debates in the United States.

The statesman and the man, Jefferson held in higher esteem although he continued to see in him the representative of a lost cause, and the Utopian cherishing an impossible and vague dream of liberty :

I have been amusing myself lately with reading the voluminous letters of Cicero. They certainly breathe the purest effusions of an exalted patriot, while the parricide Caesar is lost in odious contrast. When the enthusiasm, however, kindled by Cicero's pen and principles, subsides into cool reflection, I ask myself what

was that government which the virtues of Cicero were so zealous
to restore, and the ambition of Caesar to subvert ?... Steeped in
corruption, vice and venality, as the whole nation was, (and nobody
had done more than Caesar to corrupt it) what could even Cicero,
Cato, Brutus have done, had it been referred to them to establish
a good government for their country. (To John Adams. December 10, 1819. *M. E.* XV, 233).

For the philosopher he seems to have felt at first
a genuine admiration which changed, later in his life
into a more critical attitude. In his letter to Peter
Carr (August 19, 1785. *M. E.* V, 85), he recommends
" *in morality* " to read Cicero's philosophies, Anton-
inus and Seneca.

This admiration still holds in his *Syllabus of the
Merit of the Doctrines of Jesus, compared with those of
others* (To Benjamin Rush. April 21, 1803. *M. E.*
X, 381). " Their principles, he adds, related chiefly
to ourselves, and the government of those passions
which, unrestrained, would disturb our tranquillity
of mind. In this branch of philosophy they were
really great ". And in a foot-note he listed the
titles of Seneca's and Cicero's philosophical works,
" the most extensive we have received from the an-
cients ", and defined the purpose of each work.

He perceived however their limitations for :

In developing our duties to others, they were short and defective. They embraced, indeed, the circles of kindred and friends,
and inculcated patriotism, or the love of our country in the aggregate, as a primary obligation : towards our neighbors and coun-
trymen they taught justice, but scarcely viewed them as within the
circle of benevolence. Still less have they inculcated peace, charity and love to our fellow men, or embraced with benevolence
the whole family of mankind (*M. E.* X. 382).

True as this may be of Cicero, it is manifestly
unfair and unjust to Seneca who had at least glimpses
of the CARITAS GENERIS HUMANI and in more than one
respect was already a citizen of the world. Thus we
are led to suspect that Jefferson was not altogether

familiar with all the treatises of Seneca he had enume-
rated in his foot-note.   There is little doubt however
that Jefferson who at first was attracted by the doctrine of the Stoics, transferred his moral allegiance
to Epicurus, at a time which remains to be determined, — quite possibly under the influence of the
French « philosophes » of the Helvétius' group.   During his later years, at any rate, it is Epicurus he calls
" our master", deploring the fact that he has been
misrepresented by Cicero :

> As you say of yourself, I too am an Epicurian.   I consider the
> genuine (not the imputed) doctrines of Epicurus as containing
> everything rational in moral philosophy, which Greece and Rome
> have left us.   Epictetus indeed, has given us what was good of
> the Stoics ; all beyond, of their dogmas, being hypocrisy and gri-
> mace.   Their great crime was in their calumnies of Epicurus and
> misrepresentations of his doctrines ; in which we lament to see
> the candid character of Cicero engaging as an accomplice.   (To
> William Short. October 31, 1819. *M. E.* XV, 219).

We may now examine in a better perspective the
abstracts from Cicero copied by Jefferson.   All of
them, except one are taken from the *Tusculanæ
Quæstiones* and probably made at an early period of
Jefferson's life.   All of them are selected with a
view to confirm the deistic and materialistic tenets
which Jefferson probably held at the time.

> All must die ; if only there should be an end to misery in death
> (Lib. 1, c. 2).   What is there agreeable in life, when we must night
> and day reflect that, at some time or other, we must die ? (*Lib.* 1,
> c. 7).

A particular piece of reasoning in the *Tusculanæ*
seems to have struck very forcibly Jefferson's mind :

> For if either the heart, or the blood, or the brain, is the soul,
> then certainly the soul, being corporeal, must perish with the rest
> of the body ; if it is air, it will perhaps be dissolved ; if it is fire.
> it will be extinguished. (*Lib.* 1, c. 11).

The same view reappears in his other *Commonplace Book* (see my edition, p. 330. The Johns Hopkins Press, 1926) and again in several letters to John Adams (March 14, 1820. *M. E.* XV, 239 etc.). It was certainly in Jefferson's eyes the strongest argument ever proposed against the immortality of the soul. But if all is vanity and there is very little hope of a future life what consolation can we find in the philosophers, and what is left for men to do ?

Death which threatens us daily from a thousand accidents, and which by reason of the shortness of life, can never be far off, does not deter a wise man from making such provision for his country and his family as he hopes may last forever ; and from regarding posterity, of which he can never have any real perception as belonging to himself. (*Lib. I, c.* 38).

Thus is revealed in Jefferson an aspect of his philosophical formation that for lack of precise references has been very much neglected and even entirely ignored. We realize too little in our days the profound influence exerted by the ancient philosophers upon the minds of some of the men of the eighteenth century. This may not be altogether true of Europeans of the same period, who had at their disposal books, magazines and newspapers in abundance and were caught in the swift currents of the time. But it was undoubtedly true of a young American who had never left his native surroundings. We cannot easily determine how copious was the library of William and Mary ; we know however that the number of books available to Jefferson and his contemporaries was necessarily small and limited. The classics, that is to say the Greek and Latin authors, had not to compete with the more modern writers ; — more time was given to their perusal and they really formed the substance and constituted the intellectual foundation of most students in colleges. At least they were taken seriously by Jefferson, in them he saw more than the monuments of an abolished past and of a remote civilisation.

Many years later, Jefferson summarized thus the value of classical studies in a letter to John Brazier :

> Among the values of classical learning, I estimate the luxury of reading the Greek and Roman authors in all the beauties of their originals. And why should not this innocent and elegant luxury take its preeminent stand ahead of all those addressed merely to the senses ? I think myself more indebted to my father for this than for all the other luxuries his cares and affections have placed within my reach ; and more now than when younger, and more susceptible of delights from other sources. When the decay of age has enfeebled the useful energies of the mind, the classic pages fill up the vacuum of the grave into which we are all sooner or later to descend... A third value is in the stores of real science deposited and transmitted us in these languages, to wit : in history, ethics, arithmetic, geometry, astronomy, natural history etc (August 24, 1819. *M. E.* XV, 209).

But in his younger days the classics were to him much more than a luxury. They were his masters and counsellors ; they were the first to reveal to him the great problems of life and human conduct. In a land where religious traditions were so strong and which did not participate fully in the intellectual life of the mother country, the Bible naturally was one of the dominant influences. It was not and could not be the only one for young Americans who went to college and whose restless minds refused to accept the principle of authority. To many of them Cicero or Seneca offered new views of the nature of man, an ideal of republican liberty and devotion to one's country, a conception of wordly wisdom and political morality, and a code of ethics less sublime, but more practical and more within their reach, than the « morals of Jesus ».

THE ENGLISH WRITERS

The lessons of the classical philosophers and poets were supplemented with readings of more modern writers. Here again the selections made by Jefferson are at the same time very significant and somewhat disconcerting. Remembering the fact that he learned both French and Italian when a boy and that he is generally supposed to have been much influenced by French thought, we would naturally expect to find at least a few abstracts from the most prominent French writers. They are not wholly lacking, but their number is so small as to make them very inconclusive. Racine is the only French writer represented here : among all his tragedies Jefferson selected only ten lines from *Les Frères Ennemis*, not by any means the best of Racine's plays. Truly these abstracts cannot be indicative of Jefferson's real acquaintance with French literature. Yet if we remember that, as appears from the *Commonplace Book* I recently edited, Jefferson was not interested in the philosophical ideas of such men as Voltaire and that Montesquieu alone retained his attention, we cannot escape the conclusion that the part played by French thought on his formation, before he went to France, was after all very limited. Whatever doctrines he held in common with the " philosophes " during the early part of his life came evidently from common sources, the ancient philosophers and to a large degree from Lord Bolingbroke.

For Bolingbroke he always professed the greatest admiration as probably did many of his contemporaries. In a letter to Jefferson written in 1813, John Adams admitted that he had read Bolingbroke " for the first time fifty years ago, and not less than five times since " (December 25, 1813. *M. E.* XIV, 34). It

is not unlikely that Jefferson was introduced to the
English thinker at about the same time.

It was probably because of Bolingbroke that he
came first to question the authenticity of the Bible as
an historical document, or rather that he decided to
apply to the study of the Bible the same criterium
of evidence as to the study of the Greek and Roman
historians. The views expressed by Bolingbroke in
his *Letter to M. de Pouilly* are clearly those reproduced by Jefferson in his letter to Peter Carr :

> Question with boldness the existence of a God ; because, if
> there be one, he must more approve of the homage of reason, than
> that of blindfolded fear. You will naturally examine first, the
> religion of your own country. Read the Bible, then, as you
> would read Livy or Tacitus... (To Peter Carr, August. 10, 1787.
> *M. E.* VI, 258).

No single influence was stronger on Jefferson's
formation and none was more continuous. He
followed Bolingbroke in his distrust of metaphysical disquisitions (see *Essay 2, section 7*). He accepted his belief in some sort of a universal religion
not limited to the Jews. Most, if not all of the
ideas he expressed in his correspondence with John
Adams during the last twelve years of his life, could
be illustrated with quotations taken from the abstracts
of Bolingbroke in his commonplace book. The
years did not diminish his enthusiasm for the English
philosopher and when in 1821 Francis Eppes asked
him his opinion of Bolingbroke and Thomas Paine,
Jefferson wrote in answer a long parallel in which he
clearly expressed his preference :

> They were alike in making bitter enemies of the priests and
> pharisees of their days. Both were honest men ; both advocates
> of human liberty... Lord Bolingbroke's on the other hand, is a
> style of the highest order. The lofty, rhythmical, fullflowing
> eloquence of Cicero. Periods of just measure, their members
> proportioned, their close full and round. His conceptions, too,

are bold and strong, his diction copious, polished and commanding
as his subject. His writings are certainly the finest samples in
the English language, of the eloquence proper for the Senate. His
political tracts are safe reading for the most timid religionist, his
philosophical, for those who are not afraid to trust their reason
with discussions of right and wrong. (Jan. 19, 1821. *M. E.* XV,
305).

Pope on the other hand seems to have had but little
influence on Jefferson. The quotations from the
Essay on man are few and not particularly significant.
If we remember that in his other *Commonplace Book*
the philosophical passages are almost negligible we
must come to the conclusion that Jefferson in spite
of his reputation was not a " philosopher " not even
a " *philosophe* " in the eighteenth century sense of
the word. For abstract thinking and disinterested
speculations he cared but little. He shared Bolingbroke's confidence in human reason, but realized
very early that the realm of reason is not infinite
and does not extend beyond certain limits. And
instead of trying to solve the insoluble enigma he
then decided once for all that life was too short and
time too precious to waste his efforts in attempting
to penetrate the secret of the universe. To true
philosophers like Plato he decidedly preferred the
moralists and this appears very clearly in the abstracts
he made from Milton. *Paradise Lost* exerted on
him a very powerful attraction. He read systema-
tically through it, collecting here and there aphorisms
and moral developments, always guided in his choice
by an ultimate practical preoccupation. Neglecting
the purely poetical or theological passages he found
in *Paradise Lost* a conception of life with which he
was already familiar through his reading of the ancient Sages. It was the same *tædium vitæ*, the same
grave lamento on the brevity of life, only more solemn.
It was, finally, the same lesson of resignation to one's
fate and the same aspiration to eternal rest and sleep :

> ....How glad would lay me down
> As in my mother's lap.   There I should rest
> And sleep secure...   (*Paradise Lost*, X, 769).

Once more however when reading Milton Jefferson betrayed the same curious propensity to collect passages disparaging women. It was already quite apparent in his selections from Euripides. From the Greek dramatist he had selected with a sort of waggish pleasure the strongest denunciations of womankind and repeated with the old poet :

Mortals should beget children from some other source and there should be no womankind; thus there would be no ill for men (*Medea*, 573).

And again :

O Zeus, why hast thou established women, a curse deceiving men, in the light of the sun ?   (*Medea*, 616).

In Milton he found an echo of Euripides' antifeminism and from *Paradise Lost* and Samson Agonistes compiled a pretty set of accusations against women and female usurpations. All of which, unless we are much mistaken, would only tend to prove that these parts of his Commonplace Book were probably copied before Jefferson had fallen in love with Martha Skelton, most certainly before his marriage, that is to say before 1772. It is only the very young man or the man disappointed in love who affects this wordly-wise and cynical attitude towards women. If on the other hand we remember that after a courtship extending over two years he was jilted by Miss Rebecca Burwell, the Belinda of his letters to Page, there is at least a presumption that he took a scholarly revenge in copying from his readings what he would never have said himself to the fair one who was cruel enough to invite him to be a bridesman at her mar-

riage. There is very little likelihood that Jefferson
who never was a domestic tyrant and ·adored his
wife would have quoted after 1772 to the effect that :

> Therefore God's universal law
> Gave to man despotic power
> Over his female in due awe.(*Samson Ag.* v. 1025).

We may even venture to assert that marriage changed Jefferson's views on women. In the midst of
the quotations from Milton and separated from the
rest by a blank page are the following lines added it
seems, as an afterthought (see p. 135) :

> Nor gentle purpose, nor endearing smiles
> Wanted, nor youthful dalliance as beseems
> Fair couple, linkt in happy nuptial league,
> Alone as they...
> (Milton Paradise Lost, I, 4, v. 337).

Like so many young misogynists Jefferson had
recanted and was rejoicing in his defeat.

Of the English dramatists Skakespeare naturally
occupies the first place. Jefferson's appreciation
of him as well as his general attitude towards literature is well expressed in one of the earliest of his
letters that have been preserved. It is worth quoting
at length, for the moral preoccupation, which so
often guided Jefferson in the choice of his readings,
appears in it very conspicuously :

> We never reflect whether the story we read be truth or fiction.
> If the painting be lively, and a tolerable picture of nature, we are
> thrown into a reverie, from which if we awaken it is the fault of
> the writer. I appeal to every reader of feeling and sentiment
> whether the fictitious murder of Duncan by Macbeth in Shakes-
> peare does not excite in him as great a horror of vileny, as the real
> one of Henry IV by Ravaillac as related by Davila ? We are there-
> fore, wisely framed to be as warmly interested for a fictitious
> as for a real personage. The field of imagination is thus laid open

to our use and lessons may be formed to illustrate and carry home
to the heart every moral rule of life. Thus a lively and lasting
sense of filial duty is more effectually impressed on the mind of a
son or daughter by reading King Lear, than by all the dry volumes
of ethics and divinity, that ever were written. This is my idea
of well written Romance, of Tragedy, Comedy and Epic poetry.
(To Robert Skipwith. Aug. 3, 1771. *M. E.* IV, 238).

   Shakespeare then was, in the eyes of Jefferson essen-
tially a source of moral teachings, a profound observer
of human nature even more than a poet. This
explain why none of the comedies are mentioned,
nothing from *Romeo and Juliet*, nothing from *A Mid-
summer-night's dream*, nothing even from *The Tempest*.
It does not seem either, at least from the evidence
present in the *Commonplace Book*, that Jefferson
paid any particular attention to the political plays
of Shakespeare. He quoted from *Julius Cæsar*
and *Coriolanus*, to be sure, but, neglecting the political
maxims, he took from them only the same aristocratic
ideal of honor which had attracted him in Homer
and the Greek dramatists, and in his youthful and
eager soul echoed the lines he copied from *Henry
the Fourth* :

> But if it be a sin to covet honour
> I am the most offending soul alive.

   In his selections from more modern playwrights
Jefferson was probably directed by the same purpose.
Otway, Dryden, Congreve, Young, Rowe, Bucking-
hamshire, the adaptator of Shakespeare, are represented. Many of these quotations show the same
mysogynist bias that we have already called attention to.

> Woman the fountain of all frailty,

quotes Jefferson from *The Orphan*, which is hardly

redeemed by a single line from *Venice preserved* in which woman is praised as

Eternal joy and everlasting joy.

The latest of the contemporary poets to be mentioned by Jefferson is Thomas Moss, whose *Beggar's Petition*, published in his *Poems on several occasions*, appeared in 1769. It is typical of the sentimentality of the time, and its first line at least has long remained as a perfect example of a desuet genre :

Pity the sorrows of a poor old man...

As it was to be expected, Ossian occupies an important place among the moderns. The devotion of Jefferson to the supposed Gaelic bard is well known. In his enthusiasm he even proposed to learn the Gaelic language in order to read his favorite author in the original and rather embarrassed the worthy Mc Pherson by asking him for a copy of the poem " of this rude bard of the North, the greatest poet that has ever existed. " (see G. Chinard: *Jefferson et Ossian*. Modern Language Notes, April 1923). That he was not unaware however of the disconcerting resemblance between Ossian and the classical epics, is proved by the fact that at some later date he copied as a foot-note to a passage from Ossian lines from the *Iliad*, the *Æneid* and Statius (p. 191). Several years later however his youthful enthusiasm was unabated and when the Marquis de Chastellux visited him at Monticello, in 1782, Ossian provided the topic of their longest conversation :

I recollect with pleasure, says the Marquis, that as we were conversing over a bowl of punch, after Mrs Jefferson had retired, our conversation turned on the poems of Ossian. It was a spark of electricity which passed rapidly from one to the other ; we recollected the passages in those sublime poems which particularly struck us, and entertained my fellow-travellers, who fortunately knew English well, and were qualified to judge of their merits, though they had never read the poems. In our enthusiasm the book was sent for, and placed near the bowl, where, by their mutual aid, rthe night imperceptibly advanced upon us.

Jefferson's taste was the taste of his time. He quoted from Langhorne's *Hymn to Hope*, from Akenside's *Pleasures of Imagination*, from Mallet and Thomson and most of all from Young's *Night Thoughts* I would not go so far as to maintain that these abstracts authorize us to believe that Jefferson was contaminated by the Romantic malady then prevailing in England. They are significant however, insomuch as they indicate the readings of a young Virginian around 1770 ; they show clearly to what extent the colonies kept informed of the literary fashions of the metropolis. On the other hand it would be equally unwise to deny that the pervasive melancholy of English poetry did not awaken any echo in young Thomas Jefferson. Although his natural disposition was averse to morbid broodings, he had confessed in his letter to Robert Skipwith that "if the painting be lively and a tolerable picture of nature we are thrown into a reverie, from which if we awaken it is the fault of the writer". Poetry opened to him the portals of an enchanted world, and he even tried his hand at writing poems himself. The piece here reproduced for the first time, we believe, is given as a curiosity and not for its literary value. If according to Sainte-Beuve, most men have in them a poet who dies early, the poet in Jefferson was never born or rather remained inarticulate. The fact that the last lines are incomplete, as if the young author had been unable to find the proper rhymes and bring his effort to a satisfactory completion, is at least an indication that Jefferson wrote the poem himself and did not copy it from an anthology.

Tis hope supports each noble flame,
'Tis hope inspires poetic lays,
Our heroes fight in hopes of fame,
And poets writes (*sic*) in hopes of praise
She sings sweet songs of future years.
And dries the tears of present sorrow ;
Bids doubting mortal cease their fears,
And tells them of a bright to-morrow.
And where true love a visit pays,
The minstrell (*sic*) is always there,
To soothe young Cupid with her lays
And keep the lover from despair.
Why fades the rose upon thy cheek ;
Why drop the lilies at the view ?
Thy cause of sorrow, Ellen speak,
Why alter'd thus thy sprightly hue ?
Each day alas ! with breaking heart,
I see thy beautous form decline ;
Yet fear my anguish to impart ;
Lest it should add a pang to thine.
I will not be afraid wh.
have to

Another presumption that these abstracts were collected rather early in the life of Jefferson comes from the fact that he seems to have lost all taste for poetry shortly after 1780, if not some time before. A passage in his *Thoughts on English Prosody* is very significant in that respect :

What proves the excellence of blank verse is that the taste lasts longer than for rhyme. The fondness for the jingle leaves us with that for the rattles and baubles of childhood, and if we continue to read rhymed verse at a latter period of life it is such only where the poet has had force enough to bring great beauties of thought and diction into this form. When young any composition pleases which unites a little sense, some imagination, and some rhythm, in doses however small. But as we advance in life these things fall off one by one, and I suspect we are left at last with only Homer and Virgil, perhaps with Homer alone. He like
Hope travels on nor quits us when we die (2).

(1) Library of Congress, *Jefferson papers*, vol. I, n° 5.
(2) The manuscript of the *Thoughts on English Prosody*, written for

At about the same time he drew up a list of readings for Peter Carr and accompanied the list with a comment short but very significant :

In Greek and Latin poetry, you have read or will read at school, Virgil, Terence, Horace, Anacreon, Theocritus, Homer, Euripides, Sophocles.   Read also Milton's Paradise Lost, Shakespeare, Ossian, Pope's and Swift's works, in order to form your style in your own language.

(August 19, 1785. *M. E.* V, 85).

Some fifteen years later when John D. Burke sent him a copy of *The Columbiad* and asked him for his opinion, Jefferson refused to express any, excusing himself on the ground that :

To my own mortification... of all men living, I am the last who should undertake to decide as to the merits of poetry.   In earlier life I was fond of it and easily pleased.   But as age and cares advanced, the powers of fancy have declined.   Every year seems to have plucked a feather from her wings, till she can no longer waft one to those sublime heights to which it is necessary to accompany the poet.   So much has my relish for poetry deserted me that, at present, I cannot read even Virgil with pleasure...

(June 21, 1801. Ford edit. VIII, 65).

One may wonder however if that failure to appreciate poetry was as complete as Jefferson confessed it to be.   Ten years later, he declared to David Howell that he could hardly read one or two newspapers a week and " with reluctance *gave* even that time from Tacitus and Horace, and so much more agreeable reading " (Dec. 15, 1810. *M. E.* XII, 43).   In another

Chastellux is undated. I cannot agree with the editor of the *Memorial edition* that it was composed when Jefferson was Secretary of State. The letter which accompanies it shows clearly that it was written while Jefferson was in Paris and when the conversations he had with Chastellux at Monticello in 1782 were still fresh in his mind.

letter written to John Adams not so long after, he showed himself a perfectly competent critic of at least the poetry of the Bible :

I acknowledge all the merit of the hymn of Cleanthes to Jupiter, which you ascribe to it. It is as highly sublime as a chaste and correct imagination can permit itself to go. Yet in the contemplation of a being so superlative, the hyperbolic flights of the Psalmist may often be followed with appreciation, even with rapture ; and I have no hesitation in giving him the palm over all the hymnists of every language and of every time. (Oct. 13, 1813. *M. E.* XIII, 393).

Whatever may be the case, the Commonplace book is here to prove that at some time during the life of Jefferson he was not deaf to poetry and that he found in the British poets what he was too reticent to express himself as a personal feeling. We know that he loved music, but his appreciation of music will be better realized if we remember that he quoted from Rowe's *Fair Penitent* :

Let there be music, let the master touch
The sprightly spring, and softly breathing lute.
.........ev'n Age itself is cheer'd with Music
It wakes a glad remembrance of our Youth,
Calls back joy, and warms us into transport,

and that he collected similar passages from Milton, Shakespeare and Congreve. After the death of his dear friend Dabney Carr (1773) he sent for a plate of copper to be nailed on the tree at the foot of his grave, with this inscription taken from a passage of Mallet copied in the *Commonplace Book* :

Still shall thy grave with rising flowers be dressed
And the green turf lie lightly on thy breast ;
There shall the morn her earliest tears bestow,
There the first roses of the year shall blow,
While angels with their silver wings o'ershade
The ground sacred by thy reliques made.

He loved the trees, the forests and the hills perhaps
more than any of his American contemporaries, but
one would experi nce difficulty in finding any lyrical
expression of this love in any of his letters.   He
may have been mute in this respect, but from the hills
of Monticello he must have repeated more than once
or read again in this little book which was his confi-
dant the lines he had copied from Thomson's description of spring :

> Oft let me wander o'er the dewy fields
> Where freshness breathes, and dash the trembling drops
> From the bent bush, as thro' the verdant maze
> Of sweet-brier hedges I pursue my walk ;
> Or taste the smell of the daisy ; or ascend
> Scme eminence...
> And see the country far diffusd around,
> One boundless blush, one white-empurpled show'r
> Of mingling blossoms ; where the raptur'd eye
> Hurries from joy to joy, and hid beneath
> The fair profusion, yellow Autumn skies.

CONCLUSION

All the evidence encountered thus far tends to
establish that the larger part of the *Commonplace
Book* was written by Jefferson during an early period
of his life.   It is not likely that the man who expressed
such a profound scorn for translations whenever " the
original were obtainable " wasted his time in copying
long abstracts from Pope's translation of Homer after
he became able to read Greek easily.   A similar reasoning would apply to the abstracts of the English
poems.   Shortly after 1782, Jefferson declared that
" as we advance in life we are left only with Homer
and Virgil, perhaps with Homer alone ".   If such an
admission means anything, it can only indicate that

the quotations from Mallet, Thomson, Akenside, Thomas Moss, Edward Moore, Young and others were made at an earlier date. It is at least probable that Jefferson transcribed the passages from Ossian when he expressed such an enthusiasm for the Gaelic bard, that is to say around 1772. Finally the misogynistic trend which runs through the abstracts from Euripides to Otway is contrary to all we know of Jefferson's character after his marriage. His was certainly a marriage of love. The death of his wife struck him such a blow that he remained for a long time " in a stupor of mind " and " as if dead to the world ". When he emerged from it he did not become a hermit. He still enjoyed the society of women. He liked to write letters to them and to receive letters from them, as appears in the correspondence he kept up for many years with the vivacious Lucy Paradise, Mrs Adams, Mrs Cosway, Mme de Tessé, Mme de Corny and many others. But there is no indication that he ever fell in love again. It is hardly conceivable that the man who always treated women with an old fashioned politeness and a distinct formality, even in his private letters, would have slandered and spoiled the memory of his ten years of " unchequered happiness " by collecting the denunciations of women and married life so abundant in the Commonplace book. And yet he went through a crisis of mosigyny. His note-book for 1770 contains on the first page a Latin doggerel which indicates that two years before his marriage his distrust of women had not abated :

Crede ratem ventis, animum ne crede puellis
Namque est feminea tutior unda fide.
Foemina nulla bona est, sed si bona contigit ulla
Nescio quo fato res mala facta bona est.

Trust the winds with your bark, but do not trust the girls with your heart, for you can put your confidence more securely in the

waves than in women.   There is no good woman, and if by chance
one happens to be so, I do not know what flight of fortune changed
a bad thing into a good one.

If, on the other hand we remember that Jefferson
did not manifest any of this distrust before his
unfortunate love affair with Belinda, there is every
reason to believe that most of these quotations were
copied some time between the jilting of the young
lover and his marriage, that is to say between 1764
and 1772.   But these quotations are so closely inter-
woven with the rest of the abstracts that they cannot
be separated from them.   Thus we are justified in
assuming that with the possible exception of a few
quotations added at the end of a page or a division,
Jefferson unconsciously wrote in the Commonplace
book the confessions of his youth.

He appears in it singularly more imaginative than
in his more mature years, but the main outlines of
his personality are already plainly distinguishable.
In spite of all the quotations from ancient and modern
poets his was not a poetical mind.   Even as a student
he read more for profit than for pleasure.   Mere
picturesqueness had little attraction for him.   He
was not dreaming of a remote past and far away
lands.   In his natural dispositions there was nothing
exotic, and he deliberately swept away from his notes
everything that was unusual, strange, and, we could
almost say un-American.   Nothing is more striking
in this respect than his treatment of Horace's second
epode : *O beatus ille qui procul negotiis*... Jefferson did
not change a word of it ; but simply by omitting every
detail that was purely Roman he succeeded in lifting
out of time this picture of Roman farm life and in
changing it into a description fitting exactly America
of the colonial days.   Priapus and Silvanus have been
eliminated from the garden. Snaring rabbits or migra-
tory cranes are pleasures that a young man who never

went out without his gun would hardly appreciate ; moreover it would not be good sportsmanship, so these lines were not transcribed. The farmer's wife may well prepare for her tired husband a simple meal but wild sorrel, mallow, kid meat, or even olives would not appear on the menu, and out they went. Thus the sturdy Apulian ploughman and his good wife lost their local characteristics, the Roman farm became similar to a Southern plantation and the slaves of the household could be mistaken for American negroes playing in the yard after the day's work is done.

This is not an accident but a systematic *procédé* applied by Jefferson to most of the authors quoted in the *Commonplace Book*. If he was touched by the Romantic melancholy which pervades English poetry in the eighteenth century, he was absolutely free from primitivism and never felt that yearning to escape from one's time and one's native surroundings, which is an essential element of the Romantic soul. Such sentiments can best develop in an ancient civilization, when life becomes so complicated that man feels himself hampered and shackled by social conventions. They may have existed in New England and it is well known that the case of Thoreau's is not an isolated one ; but they could not find any sincere response in the mind of a normal young Virginian of the pre-revolutionary period. Mansions and small towns were precious islands of civilization and social life was a much desired luxury. Romanticism became an imported " fleur du mal " for the following generations ; during the late colonial days it could not take root in a virgin soil. And so Jefferson eliminated Romanticism from the Romanticists, and kept only descriptions that fitted American scenery as well as English country-side.

The fact that the problem of destiny occupies so much space in the *Commonplace Book* is no indication either of a Romantic trend. To Jefferson it was a problem of paramount importance, to be sure, but it was not to be solved by religion and even less by imagination. Governor Fauquier, the son of the Huguenot refugee who became Newton's secretary, was probably operative in bringing the problem to a definite point. Fauquier is known to have been a follower of Shaftesbury and Bolingbroke and there is a possibility that he introduced the young student of William and Mary to the works of the English philosophers. From Bolingbroke Jefferson drew the lesson that the problem of destiny must be examined in a systematical and logical way, with all the ressource made available by human reason. When he was convinced that the solution lay beyond the reach of our understanding, he bent every effort to discard the problem itself from his mind. Evidently he did not succeed at first in reaching such a pragmatic ataraxia. The *Commonplace Book* offers ample evidence that, following the reading of the ancient and modern philosophers, Jefferson went through a religious crisis. His faith in the orthodox doctrine of Christianity was profoundly shaken if not altogether destroyed.

Most adolescents who have read much and reflected somewhat pass almost necessarily through that dangerous period of self-confidence, absolute trust in the power of reason, and impatience of authority and tradition. Jefferson himself has spoken of this time of life, when he was " bold in the pursuit of knowledge, never fearing to follow truth and reason to whatever results they led, and bearding every authority which stood in their way " (*To Thomas Cooper*, Feb. 10, 1814. *M. E.* XIV, 85).

Bold as he may have been on some other matters, Jefferson however never questioned the foundations of morality, and never went as far as the English deists and the French "philosophes". Even though he refused to accept that morals rested on religious beliefs, he denied with equal emphasis, that they had their origin " in self-love, self-interest or in an aesthetic sense of fitness ". This well pronounced moral bend appears very conspicuously in this *Commonplace Book*. Homer, Euripides, Cicero were the masters who provided him with strong moral standards. " Lose no occasion to be grateful, to be generous, to be charitable, to be humane, to be true, just, firm, orderly, courageous ", he wrote to Peter Carr in 1787. Nothing in these precepts is contrary to the ideal of the " Christian gentleman ", and yet some of the essentials of that ideal are still lacking. At that time the dominant influence on the mind of. Jefferson still remained the teaching of the ancient moralists. It is only later in his life that he found in Christianity a set of moral teachings transcending the standards of antiquity. Not until 1809 will he declare that " we all agree in the obligations of the moral precepts of Jesus, and no where will they be found in greater purity than in his discourses ".

In his youth he had copied and accepted as a matter of course the statement of Bolingbroke that : " It is not true that Christ revealed an entire body of ethics, proved to be the law of nature from principles of reason and reaching all duties of life... A system thus collected from the writings of antient heathen moralists, of Tully, of Seneca, of Epictetus, and others, would be more full, more entire, more coherent, and more clearly deduced from unquestionable principles of knowledge " (*see p.* 50). To realize how far away Jefferson had drawn from such tenets it is enough to go back to the declaration he made while compiling his famous *Life and Morals of Jesus of Nazareth*, where he found " the most sublime and benevolent code of morals which has ever been offered to man ". Thus *Jefferson's Bible* may well be considered as an indirect and yet categorical recantation of Bolingbroke's haughty dogmatism. Age, experience, observation had mellowed the Stoic. He was not yet ready to accept as a whole the dogmas of Christianity, but the superiority of the morals of Jesus over the tenets of the " ·heathen moralists " did not any longer leave any doubt in his mind.

On the other hand, the questions on the hereafter that had so deeply troubled his youth came back to him in his old age. He was too much of a stoic, or better, too much of a gentleman, to let any of his younger relatives suspect that he felt any qualms before approaching death. For him it was more a matter of common decency than a matter of pride " to avoid disturbing the tranquillity of others by the expression of any opinion on the innocent questions on which we schismatize ". His letters to John Adams and Thomas Cooper reveal however that once more, during that period, Jefferson pondered over the problem of destiny without being able to find the consoling certitude he was seeking. Then he turned back to the ancient teachers who had steadied his mind and comforted him during his first philosophical crisis. From the precious little book in which he had written the psalm of life of the old poets and philosophers, he took the two melancholy lines which head his last directions for his monument :

Could the dead feel any interest in monuments or other remembrances of them, when as Anacreon says :

'Ολίγη δὲ κεισόμεσθα
Κόνις, ὀστέων λυθέντων.

A scanty dust to feed the wind
Is all the trace 't leave behind (see page 173).

It was probably at that time also that he wrote the last entry, in the book, a quotation from Quintus Smyrnaeus :

As for me I do not worry about the hereafter, even if now the doom of death stands at my feet, for we are men and cannot live forever. To all of us death must happen (see page 207).

Thus the circle was completed. The patriarch of Monticello could face death with the same courage and stoicism that had enabled the student of William and Mary to face life sixty years earlier.

The list of friends and colleagues who gave me their kind assistance would be too long to print here. Particular gratitude is due to Mr. John C. Fitzpatrick of the Manuscript Division of the Library of Congress who encouraged me to publish the *Commonplace Book* and helped me in dating the manuscript, to Miss Sites who deciphered and copied parts of it, to Professor L. Piaget Shanks who revised the introduction, to Mr. Charles Hart whose cooperation was most valuable for the translations from the Greek, and to Professors H. C. Miller and D. M. Robinson of the Johns Hopkins University.

Gilbert CHINARD.

Baltimore, June 1928.

N. B. No attempt has been made to correct Jefferson's peculiarities of spelling. Accents have been placed on Greek words, although it seems to have been Jefferson's almost constant practice to omit them entirely. Capitals have been re-established at the beginning of sentences. In other respects the manuscript is here reproduced as written by Jefferson.

HERODOTUS

The Colchians, the Egyptians, and the Ethiopians, are the only nations who have practised circumcision from the earliest times. The Phœnicians and the Syrians of Palestine themselves confess that they learnt the custom from the Egyptians.

The Egyptians were also the first to broach the opinion that the soul of man is immortal, and that when the body dies it enters into the form of another being which is born at the moment, then passing from one animal to another until it has circled through the forms of all the creatures which tenant the earth, the water and the air, after which it enters again into a human frame and is born anew. The whole period of transmigration is three thousand years.

The belief of the Getae in respect of immortality is the following. They think that they do not really die but that when they depart this life they go to Zalmoxis... But I am told that this Zalmoxis was in reality a man and was the slave of Pythagoras... and he had a chamber built in which he feasted the principal Thracians, teaching them that neither he, nor his boon companions nor any of their posterity would ever perish, but that they would all go to a place where they would live for aye in the enjoyment of every conceivable good.

(George Rawlinson's translation. London. Third edition, 1875.)

HERODOTUS

Μοῦνοι πάντων ἀνθρώπων Κόλχοι καὶ Αἰγύπτιοι καὶ Αἰθίοπες περιτάμνονται ἀπ'ἀρχῆς τὰ αἰδοῖα. Φοίνικες δέ καὶ Σύροι οἱ ἐν τῇ Παλαιστίνῃ καὶ αὐτοὶ ὁμολογέουσι παρ' Αἰγυπτίων μεμαθηνέκαι. *Compare with Gen. c.* 17, *v.* 10.

Herodot., l. 2., *c.* 104.

Πρῶτοι δὲ καὶ τόνδε τὸν λόγον Αἰγύπτιοί εἰσι οἱ εἰπόντες, ὡς ἀνθρώπου ψυχὴ ἀθανατός ἐστι· τοῦ σώματος δὲ καταφθίνοντος, ἐς ἄλλο ζῷον αἰεὶ γινόμενον ἐσδύεται. ἐπεὰν δὲ περιέλθῃ πάντα τὰ χερσαῖα καὶ τὰ θαλάσσια καὶ τὰ πετεινά, αὖτις ἐς ἀνθρώπου σῶμα γινόμενον ἐσδύνειν· τὴν περιήλυσιν δὲ αὐτῇ γίνεσθαι ἐν τρισχιλίοισι ἔτεσι.

Herodot., l. 2., *c.* 123.

Οἱ δὲ Γέται... ἀθανατίζουσι τόνδε τὸν τρόπον· οὔτε ἀποθνήσκειν ἑωυτοὺς νομίζουσι, ἰέναι τε τὸν ἀπολλύμενον παρὰ Ζάλμοξιν δαίμονα — ὡς δὲ ἐγὼ πυνθάνομαι...τὸν Ζάλμοξιν τοῦτον ἐόντα ἄνθρωπον δουλεῦσαι Πυθαγόρῃ... καὶ κατασκευάσασθαι ἀνδρεῶνα, ἐς τὸν πανδοκεύοντα τῶν ἀστῶν τοὺς πρώτους, καὶ εὐωχέοντα, ἀναδιδάσκειν ὡς οὔτε αὐτὸς, οὔτε οἱ συμπόται αὐτοῦ, οὔτε οἱ ἐκ τούτων αἰεὶ γινόμενοι ἀποθανέονται. ἀλλ᾽ ἥξουσι ἐς χῶρον τοῦτον ἵνα αἰεὶ περιεόντες ἕξουσι τὰ πάντα ἀγαθά.

Herodot., l. 4., *c.* 94, 95.

BOLINGBROKE

It is said that the sacred authors writ agreeably to all the vulgar notions of the ages and countries in which they lived, out of regard to their ignorance and to the gross conceptions of the people : as if these authors had not writ for all ages and all countries, or as if truth and error were to be followed, like fashions, where they prevailed. *Bolingbroke's philosoph. works. Essay* I. *sect.* 5.

It may be said that an extraordinary action of god on the human mind, which the word inspiration is now used to denote, is not more inconceivable, than the ordinary action of mind on body, and body on mind : and I confess that it is not. But yet the cases are so widely different, that no argument can be drawn from one in favor of the other. It is impossible to doubt of an action which is an object of intuitive knowledge, and whereof we are conscious every moment ; and it is impertinent to deny the existence of any phenomenon merely because we cannot account for it : but then this phenomenon must be apparent, and the proof that it exists, or has existed must be such as no reasonable man can refuse to admit ; otherwise we shall be exposed to make frequently the ridiculous figure that philosophers have sometimes made, when it has been discovered after they had reasoned long about a thing, that there was no such thing. *Id. Ib.*

We must not assume for truth, what can be proved. neither *à priori*, nor *à posteriori*. A mystery cannot be proved *à priori* ; it would be no mystery if it could : and inspiration is become a mystery, since all we know of it is, that it is an inexplicable action of the divine on the human mind. It would be silly, therefore, to assume it to be true, because god can act mysteriously, that is, in ways unknown to us, on his creature man : for just so Asgyll [*Asgill*] did prove, or might have proved, that men do not die but are translated, because god can translate them. There is then no possibility of proving inspiration *à priori* ; and the proofs, that are brought *à posteriori* for Christian inspiration, are not more decisive to Christians, than those, which the Stoicians brought in favor of vaticination and divination, were to them ; nor than those which the Mahometans and the worshippers of Foe bring of the same kind, are to them. *Id. Ib.*

No hypothesis ought to be maintained if a single phenomenon stands in direct opposition to it. *Id.*

If nothing which is an object of real knowledge could be opposed to the immateriality and immortality of this substance, the insuperable difficulty of accounting for the action of mind on body, and of body on mind, that are reciprocally and in their turns both active and passive, would stop our philosophical enquiries. *Id. Ib.*

Solidity and extension are the primary qualities, and in our ideas the essence of matter, of which we can frame no conception exclusively of them. What then are the primary ideas of spirit or immaterial substance ? *Id. Ib.*

It will cost a reasonable mind much less to assume that a substance known by some of it's properties may have others that are unknown, and may be capable, in various systems, of operations quite inconceivable to us, according to the designs of infinite wisdom ; than to assume that there is a substance, concerning which men do not pretend to know what it is, but merely what it is not. *Id. Ib.*

As long as matter is senseless and inert, it is not a thinking substance, nor ought to be called so. But when, in any system of it, the essential properties, extension, solidity &c. are maintained, that system is material still, tho' it become a sensitive plant, a reasoning elephant, or a refining metaphysician. It would be nonsense to assert, what no man does assert, that the idea of incogitativity can be the idea of thinking : but it is nonsense, and something worse than nonsense, to assert what you assert, that god cannot give the faculty of thinking, a faculty in the principle of it entirely unknown to you, to systems of matter whose essential properties are solidity, extension &c. not incogitativity. This term of negation can be no more the essence of matter, than that other, immateriality can be the essence of spirit. Our ideas of solidity and extension do not include the idea of thought, neither do they include that of motion ; but they exclude neither. *Id. Ib.*

Body or matter is compounded and wrought into various systems before it becomes sensible to us. We behold some that are indeed inert, senseless, stupid, and in appearance merely passive, but we behold others that have vegetative life juices and spirits that circulate and ferment in them, by which they are nourished, and by which they grow, they have not the power of beginning motion ; but motion, which is renewed in them after it has entirely ceased, and both by causes as material as themselves, continues in them, and they live, and move, and propagate their species ; till their frame is dissolved by age or sickness, or some external violence, we behold others again that have animal life, and that go from rest to motion, and from motion to rest, independently of any outward cause that determines such effects by a physical necessity in this case, as we observe to be done in the former, we discover, by the help of microscopes, an immense variety of these animal systems. Where they begin, god alone their creator and ours can tell : As these animal systems come to

be more and more sensible to us, and as our means and
opportunities of observing them increase, we discover in
them, and according to their different species, or even
among individuals of the same species, in some more in
others fewer, of the same appearances that denote a power
of thinking in us, from the lowest conceivable degrees of it,
up to such as are not far, if at all remote from those in
which some men enjoy it. I say some men, because I
think it indisputable that the distance between the intellectual faculties of different men, is often greater, than that
between the same faculties in some men and some other
animals. If now we are to form a general conclusion from
all these concurrent phenomena, without any further
reasoning about them than such as they justify, what must
it be ? It must be plainly this, that there is in the whole
animal kind one intellectual spring, common to every
species, but vastly distinguished in it's effects ; that tho'
it appears to be the same spring in all, yet it seems to be
differently tempered, and to have more elasticity and force
in some and less in others ; and that, besides this, the apparent difference in the constitutions and organizations of
animals seems to account for the different determinations
of it's motion, and the surprising variety of it's effects.
Ib. sect. 9.

The power of thinking, that very power whereof we are
conscious is as necessary to the perception of the slightest
sensation as it is to geometrical reasoning. There is no
conceivable difference in the faculty or power : the sole
difference arises from the degree in which it is or can be
exerted. *Id. Ib.*

It is absurd to affirm that a god's sovereignty good, and
at the same time almighty and alwise, suffers an inferior
dependent being to deface his work in any sort, and to
make his other creatures both criminal and miserable. *Id.*
Essay 2. *sect.* 7.

To say of a monarch in the true sense of the word, who is invested with absolute power, that he suffers one of his subjects to abuse the rest without controll, and to draw them into crimes and revolts for which he punishes them afterwards, is the most injurious accusation that can be brought. *Id. Ib.*

I combat the pride and presumption of metaphysicians in a most flagrant instance, in the assumption by which man is made the final cause of the whole creation ; for if the planets of our solar system are worlds inhabited like ours, and if the fixed stars are other suns about which other planets revolve, the celestial phenomena were no more made for us than we were for them. That noble scene of the universe, which modern philosophy has opened, gives ample room for all the planetary inhabitants, whom it leads, and even constrains us to suppose, where the spirits of the other system reside was a question easily answered, when superstition and hypothesis made up the sum of religion and philosophy. But it is not so easy to be answered now. Are the good and pure spirits in heaven ? But where is heaven ? Is it beyond all the solar systems of the universe ? or is it, like the intermundia of Epicurus, in expanses betweeen them ? Are the evil and impure spirits in hell ? But where is hell ? Is it in the center of any one planet for every system ? or is it in the center of every planet ? Do others wander in air ? or reside latent in every element ? *Id. Postscript Essay. 2.*

A polytheist who beleives one self-existent being, the fountain of all existence, by whose immediate or communicated energy all things were made, and are governed, and who looks on all those other beings whom he calls gods, that is, beings superior to man, not only as inferior to the supreme, but as beings all of whom proceed from him in several subordinate ranks, and are appointed by him to the various uses and services for which he designed them in the whole extent of the divine economy ; such a polytheist, I say, will approach nearly to true theism by holding in this manner nothing that is absolutely inconsistent with it : whilst the monotheist, who beleives that there is but one god, and ascribes to this god, whom he should conceive as an all-perfect being, the very worst of human imperfections, is most certainly ignorant of the true god and as opposite to true theism as the atheist : nay he is more injuriously so. *Id. Essay.* 3. *sect.* 1.

They who compare the ideas and notions concerning the supreme being that reason collects from the phenomena of nature, physical and moral, which we know to be the work of god, with those that the books of the old testament, which we suppose to be his word, give us, will be apt to lay these spectacles aside, and to conclude that the god of Abraham, Isaac, and Jacob, cannot be that glorious supreme all-perfect being whom reason shewed them, and whom they discerned with their naked eyes. *Id. sect.* 2.

A polytheist, who worshipping many gods, that is, inferior divinities, acknowledged still one supreme being, the monarch of gods and men, was scandalised when he saw this being, of whom he had the sublimest conceptions that the mind of man can frame, degraded into the rank of a local, tuteraly divinity, the god of Abraham, of Isaac, and of Jacob, the god of one family, and one nation, of a family who had strolled into Egypt for bread, of a nation who had been long slaves in that country. *Id. Ib.*

If we take the words of some divines that the beleif and worship of one god could be communicated no other way to mankind than by revelation,and that this sacred deposite was trusted to a people chosen to preserve it till the coming of the Messiah ; this assumption will appear as little conformable to the reason of things, as several others are which the same men advance to be parts of the divine economy and for which they appeal to the reason of mankind.

Reason will pronounce, that no people was less fit than the Israelites to be chosen for this great trust on every account. They broke the trust continually ; and the miracles, that were wrought to preserve it notwithstanding their apostasies would have preserved it at least as well all over the world. Besides, the revelations made to them were "shut up in a little corner of the world, amongst a people by that very law, which they received with it, excluded from a commerce and communication with the rest of mankind," as Mr. Locke observes very truly. A people so little known, and contemned, and thought vilely of by those nations that did know them, were therefore very "unfit, and unable to propagate the doctrine of one god in the world".

But wherefore then was this deposite made to them ? It was of no use to other nations before the coming of Christ, nor served to prepare them for the reception of his gospel ; and after his coming, it was in this great respect of little use, if of any, to the Jews themselves. They beleived universally one god, but they were not universally disposed to beleive in his son. Monotheism might indispose them to the gospel, as well as their attachment to the law of Moses. The expectation of the Messiah did not clash with monotheism but they might imagine, that the beleif of god the son, and god the holy ghost, did so very manifestly ; the trinity not having been early reconciled to the unity of god. Other nations seemed to be better prepared by philosophy, by that of Plato particularly, and by the polytheistical notions of divine natures, some in the godhead, and some out of it, for the reception of the gospel, or of the theology which the teachers of the gospel taught. Accordingly we find, that when Christ came, and threw down the wall of partition, if he did throw it down, and not St. Paul, the miracles wrought to propagate Christianity had greater effect out of Judaea than in it. On the whole matter, it is impossible to conceive, on grounds of human reason, to what purpose a divine economy, relative to the coming of Christ, should have confined the knowledge

of the true god to the Jews, and have left the rest of mankind without god in the world.   *Id. Ib.*

To recapitulate, therefore, and to conclude : I think it
plain, that the knowledge and wisdom of the one true god
must have been the religion of mankind for a long time, if
the mosaical history be authentic, and was not therefore
confined from the beginning to the family of Sem, nor to
the Israelites who pretended to be of it.   I think it plain,
that the assumed confinement of this orthodox faith and
worship could answer no imaginable design of a divine
oeconomy, preparatory to the coming of Christ ; since the
Jews who had it, were not better prepared than the Gentiles,
who are said not to have had it, to receive and embrace the
gospel ; and since this doctrine was propagated much more
by heathen philosophers than by Jewish doctors.   I think
it plain, that, if we suppose the unity of god to have been
discovered by reason, and to have been propagated by
human authority merely, the beleif of it must have gone
through all the vicissitudes, and have been exposed to all
the corruptions, that appear to have attended it.   *Id. Ib.*

When we consider the great and glorious purposes of
this revelation, the manner in which, and the person, even
the son of god himself, by whom it was made ; and all the
stupendous miracles in the heavens, and on earth, that
were wrought to confirm it ; we are ready to conclude that
such a revelation must have left reason nothing to do, but
have forced conviction, and have taken away even the
possibility of doubt.   This consequence seems so necessary,
that if such events were stated hypothetically the hypothesis would be rejected as defective and inconsistent,
unless they were supposed to have had their full effect :
and yet in fact, an universal submission of all those, who
were witnesses of the signs and wonders that accompanied
the publication of the gospel, did not follow.   The learned
men among the Jews, the scribes, the pharises, the rulers
of the people, were persecutors of christianity, not converts

to it : and the vulgar, as well as they were so far from
beleiving Jesus to be the Messiah their nation expected, or
any divine person sent by god, that when Pilate inclined
to save him, instead of Barrabbas a notorious criminal, the
whole crowd cried out, " let his blood be upon us and our
children ; " and insisted, with a sort of mutinous zeal, on
his execution.

What are we to say now ? — The infidel will insist,
that all these miracles were equivocal at best, such as
credulous superstitious persons, and none else, beleived,
such as were frequently and universally imposed by the
first fathers of the christian church, and as are so still by
their successors, wherever ignorance or superstition abound.
Essay. 4. sect. I.

If we suppose ourselves transported back to that time,
and inquiring into the truth of this revelation on the very
spot where it was made, we shall find that, far from being
determined by authority in favor of it, our reason would
have had much to do in comparing the various and contra-
dictory testimonies, and in ballancing the degrees of probability that resulted from them. *Id. sect.* 2.

We have the concurrent testimony of the sacred writers :
and it has been asked, whether we have not as much
knowledge of them as we have of several profane writers
whose histories pass for authentic ? —We read the histories of Arrian, and even of Q. Curtius, tho' we do not
know who the latter was, and the commentaries of Caesar,
as authentic histories. Such they are too for all our purposes ; and of passages which we deem genuine should be
spurious, if others should be corrupted, or interpolated,
and if the authors should have purposely, or through
deception, disguised the truth, or advanced untruth, no
great hurt would be done. But is this the case of the
scriptures ? In them, besides all the other circumstances
necessary to constitute historical probability, it is not

enough that the tenor of facts and doctrines be true ; the least error is of consequence. *Ib. Id.*

When we meet with any record cited in history, we accept the historical proof, and content ourselves with it, of how many copies soever it may be the copy. But this proof would not be admitted in judicature, as Mr. Locke observes, nor any thing less than an attested copy of the record. The application is obvious ; and if it be reasonable to take such a precaution in matters that concern private property, and wherein the sum of ten pounds may not be at stake, how much more reasonable is it to neglect no precaution, that can be taken, to assure ourselves that we receive nothing for the word of God, which is not sufficiently attested to be so ? *Id. Ib.*

The missionary of supernatural religion appeals to the testimony of men he never knew, and of whom the infidel he labors to convert never heard, for the truth of those extraordinary events which prove the revelation he preaches : and it is said that this objection was made at first to Austin the monk by Ethereld the saxon king. But the missionary of natural religion can appeal at all times, and every where, to present and immediate evidence, to the testimony of sense and intellect, for the truth of those miracles which he brings in proof : the constitution of the mundane system being in a very proper sense an aggregate of miracles. *Id. sect.* 3.

No man can beleive he knoweth not what nor why. And therefore he, who truly beleiveth, must apprehend the proposition, and must discern it's connection with some principle of truth, which, as more notorious to him, he before doth admit. Now let me ask again, can any man be said to apprehend a proposition which contains a mystery, that is, something unintelligible ; or any thing more than the sound of words ? Will not the argument against beleiving become still stronger, if a proposition is repugnant to any principles of truth, which we have before admitted on evident demonstration ? *Id. Ib.*

It is not true that Christ revealed an entire body of ethics, proved to be the law of nature from principles of reason, and reaching all the duties of life. If mankind wanted such a code, to which recourse might be had on every occasion, as to an unerring rule in every part of the moral duties, such a code is still wanting ; for the gospel is not such a code. Moral obligations are occasionally recommended and commended in it, but no where proved from principles of reason, and by clear deductions, unless allusions, parables, and comparisons, and promises and threats, are to pass for such. Where all the precepts of this kind, that are scattered about in the whole new-testament, collected, like the short sentences of antient sages in the memorials we have of them, and put together in the very words of the sacred writers, they would compose a very short, as well as unconnected system of ethics. A system thus collected from the writings of antient heathen moralists of Tully, of Seneca, of Epictetus, and others, would be more full, more entire, more coherent, and more clearly deduced from unquestionable principles of knowledge. *Id. sect. 7.*

Christianity consists
1. of the duties of Natural religion
2. duties added thereto 1. by the gospel and 2. by the church
3. articles of faith. *Id. Ib.*

If we do not acknowledge the system of belief and practise, which Jesus, the finisher as well as the author of our faith, left behind him, in the extent in which he revealed and left it, complete and perfect, we must be reduced to the grossest absurdity, and to little less than blasphemy. We assume that the son of god, who was sent by the father to make a new covenant with mankind,

and to establish a new kingdom on the ruins of paganism,
executed his commission imperfectly ; we assume, that he
died to redeem mankind from sin, and from death the wages
of sin, but that he left them at the same time without
sufficient information concerning that faith in him, and
that obedience to his law, which could alone make this
redemption effectual to all the gracious purposes of it.   In
short, we assume that they , who were converted to Christianity by Christ himself, and who died before the supposed
imperfection of his revelation had been supplied by the
apostles, by Paul particularly, lived and died without a
sufficient knowledge of the terms of salvation ; than which
nothing can be said more abominable.   — A religion,
revealed by god himself immediately, must have been
complete and perfect, from the first promulgation in the
mind of every convert to it, according to all our ideas of
order : and if we consider it as a covenant of grace, the
covenant must have been made at once, according to all
these ideas, and all those of justice.   No new articles of
belief, no new duties, could be made necessary to salvation
afterwards, without changing the covenant, and at that
rate how many new covenants might there not be ?   How
often, I say it with horror, might not god change his
mind ?   — Since these additions are made by the same
authority, and since they make a change in the covenant,
for a covenant is changed by additional conditions, tho'
the original remain still in force, the objection is confirmed.
Id. sect. 8.

The council of Laodicea admitted four gospels and rejected all the rest.   But it is very possible that this council
might proceed as councils have generally done, under the
influence of an ecclesiastical faction, and decree accordingly ; or else on some such reasons as Trenaus called a
demonstration (lib. 3.)   " There are four parts of the world.
There are four cardinal winds.   There have been four covenants, under Adam, Noah, Moses, and Christ.   There can
be but four gospels therefore. "   *It. sect.* 9.

The truth is, that as every man, in the most early days
of Christianity, judged of his own inspiration, and of
the gifts of the spirit he received, so every church judged
of the inspiration of authors, and of the divine authority
of books. The first led to the last, and these authors
were deemed inspired, and those books were canonised, in
which every particular church found the greatest conform-
ity with her own sentiments. It is astonishing to consider
how far this extravagance was carried. To consider for
instance that (1) Clement of Alexandria should look on an
Apocalypse of Peter as genuine, and it should be rejected
afterwards. That St. Paul should insert in his epistles
several passages of the apocalypse of Elias, as Origen
assures that he did, and it should be refused admittance
into the canon. But it is still more astonishing to observe
what respect Origen himself had for the visions of Hermas,
and the oracles of the Sibyl, as well as others of the fathers.
Trenaeus having cited the former, uses this expression
(lib. 4) "*scriptura pronuntiavit*" : and honest Justin, in his
admonition to the Greeks, exhorts them in a most solemn
manner to beleive the antient and venerable Sybyl, who
was extraordinarily inspired by almighty god. *Id. Ib.*

I conclude from the little that has been said on a most
voluminous subject, that as tradition furnishes very pre-
carious anecdotes to those who write at great distances of
time, so it may become difficult, nay imposible, to as-
certain the authority even of books that were written
perhaps, at the time they suppose themselves to have
been written. If the attempt to fix their authenticity, and
to reduce them into a canon, is made at a great distance of
time, they may be neither received nor rejected on grounds
absolutely sure. They may be rejected at one time, and
received at another : a remarkable example of which we
find in the adventure of the apocalypse. — The council
of Laodicea left it out of the canon in the year 860 : and

----

(1) pa. 348. line 49. *Note of Jefferson.*

altho' Asiatic bishops might pass, in this case, for judges
more competent than those of the west, the council of
Carthage put it into the canon in the year 397. *Id. Ib.*

— *wanting* —

Are contained, and by which they are all promulgated. —
the children of the first couple were certainly brothers and
sisters ; and by these conjunctions, declared afterwards
incestuous, the human species was first propagated. It
is evident on the whole, that marriages, within certain
degrees of consanguinity and affinity, are forbid by political institutions, and for political reasons ; but are left
indifferent by the law of nature, which determines nothing
expressly about them.— " Increase and multiply " is the
law of nature. The manner in which this precept shall be
executed with greatest advantage to society, is the law of
man. *Id. Fragm.* 9.

The natural reason, why marriage in certain degrees
is prohibited by the civil laws and condemned by the
moral sentiments of all nations, is derived from men's care
to preserve purity of manners ; while they reflect, that if a
commerce of love were authorised between the nearest
relations, the frequent opportunities of intimate conversation, especially during early youth, would introduce an
universal dissoluteness and corruption. But as the customs of countries vary considerably, and open intercourse
more or less restrained, between different families or between the several members of the same family, so we find
that the moral precept, varying with it's cause, is suscep-
tible, without any inconvenience, of very different latitude
in the several ages and nations of the world. The extreme
delicacy of the Greeks, permitted no converse between
persons of the two sexes, except where they lived under
the same roof ; and even the apartments of a stepmother,
and her daughters, were almost as much shut up against
visits from the husband's sons, as against those from any

strangers or more remote relations : hence in that nation it was lawful for a man to marry, not only his neice, but his half-sister by the father : a liberty unknown to the Romans and other nations, where a more open intercourse was authorized between the sexes. — Even judging of this question by the scripture, the arguments for the king's (Henry 8.) cause appear but lame and imperfect. Marriage in the degree of affinity which had place between Henry and Catherine, is indeed prohibited in Leviticus ; but it is natural to interpret that prohibition as a part of the Jewish ceremonial or municipal law : and tho' it is there said, in the conclusion, that the gentile nations, by violating these degrees of consanguinity, had incurred the divine displeasure, the extension of this maxim to every precise case before specified, is supposing the scriptures to be composed with a minute accuracy and precision, to which, we know with certainty, the sacred penmen did not think proper to confine themselves. The descent of mankind from one common father, obliged them in the first generation to marry in the nearest degrees of consanguinity : instances of a like nature occur among the patriarchs : and the marriage of a brother's widow was, in certain cases, not only permitted, but even enjoined as a positive precept by the Mosaical law. It is in vain to say that this precept was an exception to the rule ; and an exception confined merely to the Jewish nation. The inference is still just, that such a marriage can contain no natural or moral turpitude ; otherwise god, who is the author of all purity, would never, in any case, have enjoined it. *Hume's hist. Henry 8. chap. 4.*

I say that the law of nature is the law of god. Of this I have the same demonstrative knowledge,that I have of the existence of god, the all-perfect being. I say that the all-perfect being cannot contradict himself ; that he would contradict himself if the laws contained in the thirteenth chapter of Deuteronomy, to mention no others here, were his laws, since they contradict those of nature ; and therefore that they are not his laws. Of all this I have as certain, as intuitive, knowledge, as I have that two and two are equal to four, or that the whole is bigger than a part. *Bolingbroke. Fragm.* 21.

To shew, then, the more evidently how absurd, as well as impious, it is to ascribe these mosaical laws to god, let it be considered that neither the people of Israel, nor their legislator perhaps, knew any thing of another life, wherein the crimes committed in this life are to be punished ; — if Moses knew that crimes to be punished in another life he deceived the people in the covenant they made by his intervention with god. If he did not know it, I say it with horror, the consequence, according to the hypothesis I oppose, must be that god deceived both him and them. In their case, a covenant or bargain was made, wherein the conditions of obedience and disobedience were not fully, nor by consequence fairly, stated. The Israelites had better things to hope, and worse to fear, than those that were expressed in it : and their whole history seems to shew how much need they had of these additional motives, to restrain

— *wanting* —

as universal charity or benevolence was the broad foundation of their moral system. — When we consider the means of reforming mankind, which the heathen philosophers, and the christian divines had had in their turns, and compare the progress made in this great work by both, it will appear that the former had not sufficient means, not the latter a success proportionable to the means they had. In short, if Clarke's way of reasoning be good, some extraordinary and supernatural assistance to reform the world, is still wanting. *Id. Fragm.* 25.

Since the precepts and motives, offered by the best philosophers, have been never able to reform mankind, effectually, without the assistance of some higher principle, and some divine authority, nor even when both of these have been assumed, may we not be led to think that such a reformation is impracticable ? May we not conclude from the experience of all ages, that no means can bring it about, and those which have been emploied less than any ? There is a perpetual conflict in the breast of every man, who endeavors to restrain his appetites, to govern his passions, and to make reason the law of his life. Just such a conflict there is between virtue and vice, in the great commonwealth of mankind. Suppose a theist objecting to some modest reasoner *a posteriori*, who is firmly persuaded of the authenticity of the scriptures, that they contain many things repugnant to the justice and goodness of god, and unworthy of his majesty, his wisdom, and power ; the believer might reply that assurance founded on probability is the utmost which can be had in all cases of this kind ; and therefore, that he thinks himself obliged to receive these books for the word of god, tho' he cannot reconcile every thing that they contain to his ideas of the attributes of an infinite, all-perfect being. — The theist would answer — must I respect probability more than you respect certainty, and a probability which is either not established, or is established by halves ? It is not established, if the book contains any thing which implies an absolute contradiction with any conceivable perfection even of the human nature. It is established by halves, whatever external proofs you may bring, unless you can shew that the things contained in it, which seem repugnant to all our ideas of a perfect nature, are really consistent with them. *Id. fragm.* 36.

Is it agreeable to reason to beleive a proposition true, merely because it does not manifestly imply contradiction ? Is every thing that is possible, probable ? *Id. Ib.*

If the redemption be the main and fundamental article of the christian faith, sure I am, that the account of the fall of man is the foundation of this fundamental article,

and this account is, in all it's circumstances, absolutely
irreconcileable to every idea we can frame of wisdom,
justice, and goodness, to say nothing of the dignity of the
supreme being,who is introduced so familiarly, and emploied
so indecently, in taking the cool air, in making coats of
skins, to serve, instead of aprons of fig-leaves which Adam
and Eve had sewed together ; and not only in cursing the
serpent, and them, but their whole posterity, and the
world itself for their sakes. *Id. Ib.*

Did mankind stand in more need of a revelation four
thousand years after their race began than at any other
period ? *Id. Fragm.* 37.

God sent his only begotten son, who had not offended
him, to be sacrificed by men, who had offended him, that
he might expiate their sins, and satisfy his own anger.
Surely our ideas of moral attributes will lead us to think
that god would have been satisfied, more agreeably to his
mercy and goodness, without any expiation, upon the
repentance of the offenders, and more agreeably to his
justice with any other expiation rather than this. — A
heathen divine would have challenged a christian to produce
an example, in the pagan system, of a god sacrificing his
son to appease himself.   Any more than of a god who was
himself his own father and his own son — can the innocence
of the lamb of god, and the sufferings and ignominious death
of Christ, be reconcilied together ? — Let us suppose a
great prince governing a wicked and rebellious people.   He
has it in his power to punish,he thinks fit to pardon them.
But he orders his only and beloved son to be put to death
to expiate their sins, and to satisfy his royal vengeance.
Would this proceeding appear to the eye of reason and in
the un-

— wanting —

on it, and requires no broader foundation — What now has
artificial theology pretended to add to that knowledge of

the deity, which natural theology communicates ? It
pretends to connect, by very problematical reasonings *a
priori* moral attributes, such as we conceive them, and
such as they are relatively to us, with the physical attributes
of god ; tho there be no sufficient foundation for this proceeding in the phaenomena of nature : nay, tho the phaenomena are in several cases repugnant. God is just, and
good, and righteous, and holy, as well as powerful and
wise. — Such were their notions. *Id. Ib.*

Man is the principal inhabitant of this planet, a being
superior to all the rest.   But will it follow from hence, that
the system, wherein this planet rolls, or even this planet
alone, was made for the sake of man ?   Will it follow that
infinite wisdom had no other end in making man, than
that of making an happy creature ? Surely not. The
suppositions are arbitrary, and the consequences absurd.
There is no pretence to say that we have any more right
to complain of the evils which affect our state than our
fellow creatures of the evils which affect theirs, or which
are common to both. Because god has given us intellectual powers superior to theirs — is he cruel and unjust
because he has not given us invulnerable and impeccable
natures ?— Modern discoveries in astronomy have presented the works of god to us in a more noble scene. We
cannot doubt that numberless worlds and systems of
worlds compose this amazing whole, the universe ; and as
little, I think, that the planets, which roll about our sun,
or those which roll about a multitude of others, are inhabited by living creatures fit to be the inhabitants of them.
When we have this view before our eyes, can we be
stupid or impertinent and vain enough to imagine, that
we stand alone, or foremost among rational created beings ;
we, who must be conscious — of the imperfection of our
reason ? shall we not be persuaded rather, that as there
is a gradation of sense and intelligence here from animal
beings imperceptible to us for their minuteness, without
the help of microscopes, and even with them, up to man,

in whom, tho this be their highest stage, sense and intelligence stop short and remain very imperfect; so there is a gradation from man, through various forms of sense, intelligence, and reason, up to beings who cannot be known by us because of their distance from us, and whose rank in the intellectual system is even above our conceptions : — Let me ask now the greatest flatterers of human nature, what proportion there is between the excellencies of it, and the goodness of god, that should determine his infinite wisdom to judge it essential to his goodness, when he resolved to make man, to make a planet the more for this ideal creature ? The habitation is fit for him, and he is fitted to live in it. He could not exist in any other. But will it follow, that the planet was made for him, not he for the planet ? The ass would be scorched in Venus or Mercury, and be frozen in Jupiter or Saturn. Will it follow that this temperate planet was made for him, to bray and to eat thistles in it ? *Id. Frag.* 42.

To chuse the best end, and to proportion the means to it, is the very definition of wisdom, two things are then evident. One, that, since infinite wisdom determined to call into existence every being that does exist, and to constitute that universal system, which we call the system of nature, it was right and fit that infinite power should be exercised fot this purpose. The other, that, since infinite wisdom not only established the end, but directed the means, the system of the universe must be necessarily the best of all possible systems : which it could not be, nor even a consistent scheme, unless the whole was the final cause of every part, and no one nor more parts the final causes of the whole. — Why does the rain pour down into the sea, whilst the sandy deserts of Lydia are parched with drought ? Why do wintry storms happen in the summer, and irregular seasons destroy our harvests ? Such questions as these have been often asked and all of them relatively to man. They have been answered in many instances by new discoveries after the deaths of those who asked them : and posterity has been convinced, tho they did not live to be so, that when they triumphed in them, they [triumphed in their ignorance].

— wanting —

several rites of external devotion : and to keep up a belief that they are few, and that the providence of god, as it is exercised in this world, is therefore on the whole unjust, serves to keep up the belief of another world, wherein all, that is amiss here, shall be set right.   The ministry of a clergy is thought necessary on both these accounts by all. *Id. frag: 55.*

Nothing can be less reconcileable to the notion of an all-perfect being, than the imagination that he undoes by his power in particular cases what his wisdom, to whom nothing is future, once thought sufficient to be established for all cases. *Id. Ib.*

Who are to be reputed good Christians ?   Go to Rome, they are papists.   Go to Geneva, they are Calvinists.   Go to the north of Germany, they are Lutherans.   Come to London, they are none of these.   Orthodoxy is a mode. It is one thing at one time and in one place.   It is something else at another time, and in another place, or even in the same place : for in this religious country of ours, without seekings proofs in any other, men have been burned under one reign, for the very same doctrines they were obliged to profess in another.   You damn all those who differ from you.   We doubt much about your salvation.   In what manner, now, can the justice of god be manifested by particular providences ?   Must the order of them change as the notions of orthodoxy change, and must they be governing them ?   If they are favorable to those of your communion, they will be deemed unjust by every good protestant, and god will be deemed unjust by every good papist, and god will be taxed with nursing up heresy and schism. God can do nothing more, than to furnish arms against himself, by the dispensations of particular providences in the christian world ; and every one of these will pass in the minds of some men for a proof of injustice, if it passes in the minds of others for a proof of justice. *Id. frag.* 57.

If providences were directed according to the different desires, and even wants of men, equally well entitled to the divine favor, the whole order of nature, physical and moral, providences are exercised so rarely, so secretly, or some h[ow] or other so ineffectually, that his government continues liable to the same charge of injustice, and cannot be reconciled to his attributes, without the help of another hypothesis. *Id. frag.* 62.

That a due proportion of reward and punishment, that reparation and terror, are objects essential to the constitution of human justice, will not be denied. That which falls short of these is partial : that which goes beyond t[hem] cruel. Men are liable to err on both sides : god on neither. Men may have, therefore, amends to make ; god never c[an] and when we say amends have been made, we imply that injustice has been committed. Now, as absurd as appears to say this when we speak of the proceedings of god towards good men in the other life, we must say [it] for we have nothing else to say, if we assume that he has dealt unjustly by them in this life ; since it is beyond omnipotence to cause that, which has been done, not to have been done. The happy state of good men in heaven according to this bold hypothesis, is not so much the reward of the virtue they practised on earth, as an act of god's justice against himself, as it were ; an act, in short, by which he makes them reparation, and an ample on[e] it is, for the injustice he did them here. The miserable state of wicked men in hell is an exercise of justice delayed, but exercised so severely at last, that it would exceed vastly all the necessary degrees of terror, if any of these creatures remained after it in an undetermined condition wherein terror might have it's effect. — Justice requires that punishments, and we must say the same of rewards, the two sanctions of all laws, be measured out in various degrees and manners, according to the various circumstances of particular cases, and in a due proportion to them. —I ask the men who maintain that justice is the same in god as it is in our ideas of it, and who presume, on these ideas, to censure the divine providence when they see such as they esteem good involved sometimes in publik calamities with such as they esteem wicked, whether this be a jot more repugnant to their ideas of justice and of the moral fitness of things, whereon they insist so much, than it is to reward the greatest and the least degr[ee] of virtue, and to punish the greatest and the least degree of vice, alike ? The particular rules of justice consist in the distinction and proportion that have been mentioned and unless they are preserved, the general rules must be of course perverted. I ask what these persons would say if they beheld a man, who had done some trifling good to society, recompensed like one who had saved his country or if they, who were convicted of petty larceny, should be delivered over to the hangman, at one of our sessions, with those who had been found guilty of assassination and robbery. *Id. fragm. 6s.*

If the immortality of the soul could be proved by physical arguments, the eternity of rewards and punishments would be no necessary corollary deducible from it. But this immortality is a consequence necessarily deducible from this eternity. This immortality therefore, seems to rest on a moral proof, and an inverted order of reasoning, since if the justice of god requires that there should be a state of eternal rewards and punishments, the soul of man is immortal certainly. *Id. frag.,* 69.

Compare the greatest human virtue you can imagine, exposed to all the calamities of life during a term of fifty

or threescore years, and recompensed with happiness
which exceeds vastly in every instance of it, as much as
in it's duration, the sum total of all these calamities, that
is, with happiness infinite and eternal. Compare the
greatest human wickedness you can imagine, accompanied
with an uninterrupted unmingled effluence of every thing
which can go to the constitution of human felicity during
the same number of years, and after that punished in a
state of excessive and never-ending torments. What
proportion, in the name of god, will you find between the
virtue and the recompense, between the wickedness and
the punishment ?   One of these persons has amends made
to him beyond all conceivable degrees of a just reparation.
The other has punishment inflicted on him beyond all
conceivable degrees of a necessary terror again.   Suppose
two men of equal virtue, but of very opposite fortunes in
this life ; the one extremely happy, the other as unhappy
during the whole course of it.   Are these men recompensed
alike in the next ?   If they are, there arises such a disproportion of happiness in favor of one of these virtuous men,
as must appear inconsistent with justice, and can be
imputed to nothing but partiality, which theism will never
impute to the supreme being, whatever artificial theology
may do, and does in many instances.   Are these two
men not recompensed alike ?   Has one of them a
greater, and the other a less, share of happiness in that
heaven to which they both go ?   If this be said and
allowed, the same disproportion, nay, a disproportion
infinitely greater, will remain.   The difference must be
made by the degree, it cannot be made by the duration, of
this happiness, which both of them are to enjoy eternally,
not any degree of happiness the more, tho' never so small,
enjoyed eternally, will exceed infinitely not only all the
happiness of earth, but all that of heaven which can be
enjoyed in any determined number of years.   If you
suppose two persons of equal guilt, one of whom has been
as happy as a wicked man can be, and the other of whom
has suffered as much misery in this life as a wicked man

can be thought to deserve ; the same reasoning will hold good : the disproportion of punishments in one case will be like the disproportion of rewards in the other ; and that justice, which is said to be the same in god as in our ideas, will be acquitted in neither. *Id. fragm.* 69.

To reform offenders is neither the sole, nor the principal end of punishments. Those of an inferior kind may have this intention. Those that are capital must have some other : and it would be too ridiculous to make the hangman, who executes a criminal, pass for the reformer of his manners. The criminal is executed for the sake of others, and that he, who did much hurt in this life, may not only be deprived of the power of doing any more, but may do some good' too by the terror of his death.— But what effect of this kind can further punishments have when the system of human government is at an end ; and the state of probation over ; when there is no further room for reformation of the wicked, nor reparation to the injured by those who injured them ; in fine, when the eternal lots of all mankind are cast, and terror is of no further use ? *Id, frag.* 70.

Natural religion represents an all perfect being to our adoration and to our love ; and the precept " thou shalt love the lord thy god with all thy heart; will be effectual in this system. —Can any man now presume to say that the god of Moses, or the god of Paul, is this amiable being? The god of the first is partial, unjust, and cruel ; delights in blood, commends assassinations, massacres and even exterminations of people. The god of the second elects some of his creatures to salvation, and predestinates others to damnation, even in the womb of their mothers. *Id. fragm.* 81.

Tho we cannot strictly speaking, have a certain knowledge of any fact whereof we have not been ourselves witnesses, yet are there several such facts whereof we

cannot doubt. High probability must stand often in lieu
of certainty ; or we must be, every moment, at a loss how
to form our opinions and to regulate our conduct. Such is
our condition ; and we cannot think it unreasonably imposed, since we are able by a right use of our reason, to
ascend through various degrees from absolute improba-
bility, which is little distant from evident falsehood to that
degree of probability which is little distant from evident
truth.— An historical fact which contains nothing that
contradicts general experience, and our own observation,
has already the appearance of probability ; and if it be
supported by the testimony of proper witnesses, it acquires
all the appearances of truth ; that is, it becomes really
probable in the highest degree. A fact on the other
hand, which is repugnant to experience, shocks us from
the first ; and if we receive it afterwards for a true fact,
we receive it on outward authority, not on inward conviction. Now to do so is extremely absurd ; since the same
experience, that contradicts this particular fact, affirms this
general fact, that men lie very often, and that their authority alone is a very frail foundation of assent — A fact
may be indifferent. We may discover in our experience,
none of the same sort ; and yet none that imply contradi-
tion, with it. Such a fact, therefore, is merely new ; and
experience will be far from teaching us to reject any fact
on this account alone. When such facts, therefore, new
to us, according to the extent of our knowledge, but not
so to other men, are attested by credible witnesses, he must
act very unreasonably, who refuses to give that degree of
assent to them, which is proportionable to the credibility
of the witnesses. Again, the fact may be conformable
to experience by a certain analogy physical or moral, if
not by particular examples ; and may be admitted therefore,
on proper testimony : more easy still, than one of those
which I called indifferent. One rests wholly on testimony,
but experience gives to the other an indirect, if not a direct
confirmation. A story circumstantially related, ought not
to be received on the faith of tradition ; since the least

reflection on human nature is sufficient to shew how unsafely a system of facts and circumstances can be trusted for it's preservation to memory alone, and for it's conveiance to oral report alone ; how liable it must be to all those alterations, which the weakness of the human mind must cause necessarily, and which the corruption of the human heart will be sure to suggest. — History has this advantage over tradition : the authors of authentic history may be known ; but those of tradition, whether authentic or unauthentic, are not known. The probability of facts must diminish by length of time, and can be estimated, at no time, higher than the value of that original authority from which it is derived. This advantage then authentic history has, which no tradition can have. The degree of assent which we give to history may be settled in proportion to the number, character, and circumstances of the original witnesses ; the degree of assent to tradition cannot be so settled. — We are deceived, grossly, very often about the number of witnesses, two ways. Sometimes by applying testimonies that have no relation to the thing testified, and sometimes by taking different repetitions of the same testimony, for different testimonies. —History to be authentic must give us not only the means of knowing the number but of knowing the character of the witnesses who vouch for it. — When the motives and designs of authors are not the same, when they had no common principle, and when they cannot be suspected to have had any concert together nothing but a notoriety of facts can make their relation coincide. — Common sense requires that every thing proposed to the understanding should be accompanied with such proofs as the nature of it can furnish. He who requires more, is guilty of absurdity. He who requires less, of rashness. As the nature of the proposition decides what proofs are exigible and what not, so the kind of proof determines the class into which the proposition is to be ranged. *Id. Letter to Mr. de Pouilly.*

Tillotson says : " I ask no more, than that the same credit may be to Moses, as we give to every other historian. Now this cannot be reasonably refused, since he is quoted by the most antient heathen historians, and since the antiquity of his writings has never been contested by any of them, as Josephus maintains. " This is my text. I shall make some few remarks upon it, and this general remark in the first place : it has been said truly enough that the court of Rome has established many maxims and claims of right, by affirming them constantly and boldly against evident existent proofs of the contrary. The jewish and the christian church have proceeded by the same rule of policy : and the authority of the pentateuch, to say nothing here of the other books of the old testament, has been established entirely and solely on affirmation, the affirmation of the Jews ; or, at best, on seeming, and equivocal proofs, such as Josephus brings ; against such evident marks of falsehood as can be objected to no other writings, except to professed romances, nor even allways to them.—

To constitute the authenticity of any history, these are some of the conditions necessary. 1. It must be writ by a contemporary author, or by one who had contemporary materials in his hands. 2. It must have been published among men who are able to judge of the capacity of the author, and of the authenticity of the memorials on which he writ. 3. Nothing repugnant to the universal experience of mankind must be contained in it. 4. The principal facts at least, which it contains, must be confirmed by collateral testimony, that is, by the testimony of those who had no common interest of country, of religion, or of profession, to disguise or falsify the truth.

1. That Moses was not a contemporary author is allowed; and that he could have no contemporary authority for the greatest part of what he advanced concerning the creation, is proved. (for had Moses taken his materials from the mouth of Adam himself, they would not have been sufficient vouchers of what passed on the five first days, wherein the

whole material world was created.)   2.   Were the writings
of Moses published among people able to judge of them
and of their author ?   A book, ·to be deemed authentic,
must have been received, as such, in the age which followed
immediately the publication of it, and in all the ages which
followed this.   Has it been sufficiently proved that the
Mosaical history was so received ?   I believe not.   3.
Things repugnant to the experience of mankind are to be
found in many histories which pass however for authentic ;
in that of Livy for instance, but then these incredible
anecdotes stand by themselves as it were, and the history
may go on without them.   But this is not the case of the
pentateúch, nor of the other books of the old testament.
Incredible anecdotes are not mentioned seldom and
occasionally in them the whole history is founded on such,
it consists of little else, and if it were not an history of
them, it would be an history of nothing.   — Two or
three incredible anecdotes, in a decade of Livy, are easily
passed over : I reject them, and I return, with my author,
into the known course of human affairs, where I find
many things extraordinary, but none incredible.   I cannot
do this in reading the history of the old testament.   It is
founded in incredibility.   Almost every event contained
in it is incredible in it's causes or consequences : and I
must accept or reject the whole, as I said just now.   I can
do no otherwise, if I act like an indifferent judge, and if
I give no more credit to Moses than to any other historian.
— 4. An history is deemed to be true, when other contemporary, or nearly contemporary histories relate the same
fact and in the same manner.   But if the authors of these
books had a common interest of country, of religion, or of
profession, to disguise or falsify the truth, all these testimonies would be in effect but one ; as all those of the old
testament, which confirm the mosaical history are in
truth but one, the testimony of Moses himself.   — Whenever any circumstance is found in profane history or
tradition that has any seeming relation to sacred history,
it is produced as a collateral testimony ; and sometimes

even the similitude of sounds is emploied for the same
purpose, with a great apparatus of learning. But nothing
can be more impertinent than this learning. — That the
Israelites had a leader and legislator called Moses, is
proved by the consent of foreign[ers] whom I call collateral
witnesses. Be it so. But surely it will not follow that
this man conversed with the supreme being face to face ;
which these collateral witnesses do not affirm. The Israelites were an egyptian colony, and conquered Palestine.
Be it so. It will not follow that the red sea opened a
passage to them, and drowned the Egyptians who pursued
them. It will not follow, that the possession of the land
of Canaan was promised to their father Abraham four
hundred years before, as a consequence of the vocation of
this patriarch, and of an alliance which god made with
him and his family. — The most excellent constitutions
of human government and systems of human law become
often useless, and even hurtful either in a natural course
of things, or by extraordinary conjunctures, which the
wisdom of legislators could not foresee, one of the most
conceivable perfections of a law is, that it be made with
such a foresight of all possible accidents, and with such
provisions for the due execution of it in all cases, that the
law may be effectual to govern and direct these accidents
instead of lying at the mercy of them. — Another of the
most conceivable perfections of a law consists in the clear-
ness and precision of it's terms. — Tho' this is ideal, not,
real perfection among men, it will be found, no doubt, and
ought to be expected, when god is the legislator. — On
the first head, we cannot read the bible without being
convinced that no law ever operated so weak and so uncertain in effect as the law of Moses did. Far from prevailing against accidents and conjunctures, the least was
sufficient to interrupt the course, and to defeat the designs,
of it : to make that people not only neglect the law, but
cease to acknowledge the legislator. — If this be ascribed
to the hardness of heart and obstinacy of the people, in
order to save the honor of the law, this honor will be

little saved and it's divinity ill maintained.   This excuse
might be admitted in the case of any human law ; but we
speak here of a law supposed to be dictated by divine
wisdom, which ought, and which would have been able,
if it had been such, to keep in a state of submission to it,
and of national prosperity, even a people rebellious and
obstinate enough to break through any other.   — On the
second head : the language in which this law was given is,
the learned say, of any languages, the most loose and
equivocal ; and the style and manner of writing of the
sacred authors, whoever they were, or whenever they lived,
increased the uncertainty and obscurity even of any
other language how should it be otherwise, when the same
passages may be taken in historical, mystical, liberal, and
allegorical, senses ; and when those who writ them knew so
little what they writ, that they foretold so[me] future, when
they imagined they were relating so[me] past event.   —
There may be some defects in hu[man] laws, some falsities
or mistakes in human histories, and yet both of them may
deserve all the respect and all the credit, on the whole,
that the writing of fallible men can deserve, but any one
defect and one falsity, or mistake, is sufficient to shew
the fraud and imposture of writings that pretend to contain the infallible word of god.   Now there are gross defects and palpable falsehoods, in almost every page of the
scriptures, and the whole tenor of them is such as no man
who acknowleges a supreme all-perfect being [c]an beleive
to be his word.   This I must prove.   —Moses, they say,
was divinely inspired ; and yet Moses as ignorant of the true
system of the universe, as any of the people of his age.
— To evade the objection we are told that he conformed
himself to the ignorance of the people.   He did not write
to instruct the Israelites in natural philosophy, but to
imprint strongly on their minds a belief of one god, the creator of all things.   Was it necessary to that purpose that
he should explain to them the Copernican system ?   No,
most certainly.   But it was not necessary to this purpose
neither, that he should, give them an absurd account,

since he thought fit to give them one, of the creation of
our physical, and we may say, of our moral system.   It
was not necessary, for instance, he should tell them that
[the light was created... the sun, the moon, and the
stars] (1).

— *wanting* —

(1) *Bolingbroke* : *A letter occasioned by one of Archbishop Tillotson's
Sermons.*

CICERO (1)

Honor nourishes the arts, and glory is the spur to all studies ; these are always neglected in every nation which are looked upon disparagingly.

All must die ; if only there should be an end of misery in death.

What is there agreeable in life, when we must night and day reflect that, at some time or other, we must die ?

For if either the heart, of the blood, or the brain, is the soul, then certainly the soul, being corporeal, must perish with the rest of the body ; if it is air, it will perhaps be dissolved ; if it is fire, it will be extinguished.

And this may further be brought as an irrefragable argument for us to believe that there are Gods — that there never was any nation so barbarous, nor any people in the world so savage, as to be without some notion of gods. Many have wrong notions of the Gods, for that is the nature and ordinary consequence of bad customs, yet all allow that there is a certain divine nature and energy. Nor does this proceed from the conversation of men, or the agreement of philosophers ; it is not an opinion established by institutions or by laws ; but, in every case the consent of all nations is to be looked upon as a law of nature.

And the error prevailed so much, that although men knew that the bodies of the dead had been burned, yet they conceived such things to be done in the infernal regions as could not be executed or imagined without a body.

(1) C. D. Yonge's translation in *Harper's Classical Library*.

[CICERO]

Honos alit artes : omnesque incenduntur ad studia
gloriâ : jacentque ea semper, quæ apud quosque impro-
bantur. *Cic. Tusc. Quaest. Lib.* i. [2]

Moriendum est enim omnibus : esset tamen miseriæ·
finis in morte. *Id.* [I, 4]

Quæ enim potest in vita esse jucunditas, cum dies, et
noctes cogitandum sit, jam jamque esse moriendum ? *Id.*
[*I*, 7]

Nam si cor, aut sanguis, aut cerebrum est animus, certe,
quoniam est corpus, interibit cum reliquo corpore : si
anima est, fortasse dissipatur si ignis extinguitur. *Id.*
[*I*, 11]

Ut porro firmissimum hoc afferi videtur, cur Deos esse
credamus, quod nulla gens tam fera, nemo omnium tam
sit immanis, cujus mentem non imbuerit Deorum opinio.
Multi de Diis prava sentiunt : id enim vitioso more effici
solent : tamen esse vim, et naturam divinam arbitrantur.
Nec vero id collocutio homimum, aut consessus efficit non
institutis opinio est confirmata, non legibus.   Omni autem
in re consensio omnium gentium, lex naturæ putanda est.
Id. [*I.*, 13]

Tantumque valuit error,...... ut corpora cremata cum
scirent, tamen ea fieri apud inferos fingerent, quæ·
sine corporibus nec fieri possunt, nec intelligi.   *Id.* [I, 16]

And they must needs have these appeareances speak, which is not possible without a tongue, and a palate, and jaws, and without the help of lungs and sides, and without some shape or figure.

For that God who presides in us forbids our departure hence without his leave. But when God himself has given us a just cause, as formerly he did to Socrates, and lately to Cato, and often to many others, in such case, certainly every man of sense would gladly exchange this darkness for that light ; not that he would forcibly break from the chains that held him, for that would be against the law ; but, like a man released from prison by a magistrate or some lawful authority, so he too would walk away, being released and discharged by God.

For what else is it that we do, when we call off our minds from pleasure, that is to say, form our attention to the body, from the managing our domestic estate, which is a sort of handmaid and servant of the body, or from duties of a public nature, or from all other serious business whatever ? What else is it, I say, that we do, but invite the soul to reflect on itself ? oblige it to converse with itself, and as far as possible break off its acquaintance with the body ? Now to separate the soul from the body, is to learn to die, and nothing else whatever. Wherefore take my advice ; and let us meditate on this and separate ourselves as far as possible from the body, that is to say, let us accustom ourselves to die. This will be enjoying a life like that of heaven even while we remain on earth.

Death, then, which threatens us daily from a thousand accidents, and which, by reason of the shortness of life, can never be far off, does not deter a wise man from making such provision for his country and his family as he hopes may last forever ; and from regarding posterity, of which he can never have any real perception, as belonging to himself.

Has autem imagines loqui volunt : quod fieri nec sine lingua, nec sine palato, nec sine faucium, laterum, pulmonorum vi, figura potest. *Id*. [*I*, 16]

Vetat enim dominans ille in nobis injussu hinc nos suo demigrare. Cum vero causam justam Deus ipse dedeiit, ut tunc Socrati, nunc Catoni, sæpe multis : ne ille medius fidius vir sapiens, lætus ex his tenebris in lucem illam excesserit nec tamen illa vincula carceris ruperit : leges enim vetant : sed tanquam a magistratu, aut ab aliqua potestate legitima, sic a Deo evocatus, atque emissus exierit *Id*. [*I*, 30].

Quid aliud agimus, cum a voluptate, id est a corpore, cum a re familiari, quæ est ministra et famula corporis, cum a Rep. cum a negotio omni sevocamus animum ? Quid, inquam, tum agimus, nisi animum ad se ipsum advocamus, secum esse cogimus, maximeque a corpore abducimus ? Secernere autem a corpore animum, necquicquam aliud est, quam mori discere. Qua re hoc commentemur mihi crede, disjungamusque nos a corporibus, id est consuescamus mori. Hoc est dum erimus in Terris, erit illi cœlesti vitæ simile. *Id*. [*I*. 31]

Itaque non deterret sapientem mors, quæ propter incertos casus quotidie imminet propter brevitatem vitæ nunquam non longe potest abesse, quo minus in omne tempus Reip. suisque consulat, ut posteritatem ipsam, cujus sensum habiturus non sit, ad se putet pertinere. *Id*. [*I*. 38].

For although there be nothing in glory to make it desirable, yet it follows virtue as its shadow.

For this present life is really death, which I could say a good deal in lamentation for if I chose.

For if that last day does not occasion an entire extinction, but a change of abode only, what can be more desirable ?   And if it, on the other hand, destroys, and absolutely puts an end to us, what can be preferable to having a deep sleep fall on us, in the midst of the fatigues of life, and beeing thus overtaken, to sleep to eternity ?

For whoever dreads what cannot be avoided can by no means live with a quiet and tranquil mind.   But he who is under no fear of death, not only because it is a thing absolutely inevitable, but also because he is persuaded that death itself hath nothing terrible in it provides himself with a very great resource towards a happy life.

There is in the soul of every man something naturally soft, low, enervated in a manner and languid.   Were there nothing besides this, men would be the greatest of monsters ; but there is present to every man reason, which presides over and gives laws to all ; which by improving itself and making continual advances, becomes perfect virtue.   It behooves a man, then to take care that reason shall have the command over that part which is bound to practice obedience.

We are not the offspring of flints ; but we have by nature something soft and tender in our souls, which may be put into a violent motion by grief, as by a storm.

The seeds of virtue are natural to our constitutions, and, were they suffered to come to maturity, would naturally conduct us to a happy life ; but now, as soon as we are born and received into the world, we are instantly familiarized with all kinds of depravity and perversity of opinions ; so that we may be said almost to suck in error with our

Etsi enim nil in se habeat gloria, cur expectatur tamen virtutem tanquam umbra sequitur. *Id.* [I, 45] :

Nam hæc quidem vita, mors est : quam lamentari possem, si liberet. *Id.* [*I.* 31]

Nam si supremus ille dies non extinctionem, sed commutationem affert loci, quid optabilius ? Sin autem peremit, ac delet omnino, quid melius, quam in mediis vitæ laboribus obdormiscere. et ita conniventem somno consopiri sempiterno ? *Id.* [*I*, 49]

Nam qui id, quod vitari, non potest, metuit is vivere animo quieto non potest : sed qui, non modo quia necesse est mori, verum etiam quia nîl habet mors quod sit horrendum, mortem non timet, magnum is sibi præsidium ad beatam vitam comparat. *Id. Lib.* 2. [1 *I*].

Est in omnium fere natura molle quiddam demissum, humile, enervatum quodam modo, et languidum. Si nihil esset aliud, nihil esset homine deformius. Sed præsto est domina omnium, et regina ratio, quae conixa per se, et progressa longius, fit perfecta virtus. Hæc ut imperet illi parti animi, quæ obedire debet, id videndum est viro. *Id.* [*II*, 21].

Non enim silice nati sumus : sed est, natura in animis tenerum quiddam, atque molle, quod aegritudine, quasi tempestate, quatiatur. *Id. Lib.* 3. [6].

Sunt enim ingeniis nostris, semina innata virtutum quæ si adolescere liceret, ipsa nos ad beatam vitam natura perduceret. Nunc autem, simul atque editi in lucem, et suscepti sumus, in omni continuo pravitate et et in summa opinionum perversitate versamur, ut pene cum lacte nutricis errorem suxisse videamur. Cum vero

nurse's milk. When we return to our parents, and are
put into the hands of tutors and governors, we are imbued
with so many errors that truth gives place to falsehood, and
nature herself to established opinion.

The whole cause, then, is in opinion ; and this observation
applies not to this grief alone, but to every other disorder
of the mind.

Now we should exert our utmost efforts to oppose these
perturbations, which are, as it were, so many furies let
loose upon us and urged on by folly, if we are desirous
to pass this share of life that is allotted to us with ease
and satisfaction.

For there is nothing that breaks the edge of grief and
lightens it more than considering, during one's whole life,
that there is nothing which it is impossible should happen,
or than, considering what human nature is, on what
conditions life was given, and how we may comply with
them. The effect of which is that we are always grieving,
but that we never do so.

Whoever, then, through moderation and constancy, is at
rest in his mind, and in calm possession of himself, so as
neither to pine with care, nor be dejected with fear, nor to
be inflamed with desire, coveting something greedily, nor
relaxed by extravagant mirth — such a man is that
identical wise man whom we are inquiring for : he is the
happy man, to whom nothing in this life seems intolerable
enough to depress him ; nothing exquisite enough to
transport him unduly.

That there are other things more pleasant to say, I
know it ; but even if did not prompt me to say what is true
rather than what is plesant, necessity would compel me.
I would well wish to please you, Quirites, but I had far
sooner your should be saved whatever your feelings towards
me may be in the future.

parentibus redditi, id est magistris traditi sumus, tum ista variis imbuimur erroribus, ut vanitati veritas, et opinioni confirmata natura ipsa cedat. *Id.* [*II,1*]

Est causa omnis in opinione, nec vero ægritudinis solum, sed etiam reliquarum omnium perturbationum. *Id.* [*III*, 11].

His autem perturbationibus, quas in vitam hominum stultitia quasi quasdam immittit furias, atque incitat omnibus viribus : atque opibus repugnandum est si volumus hoc, quod datum est vitæ, tranquille, placideque traducere. *Id.* [*III*, 11].

Nihil est enim, quod tam obtundat, elevetque ægritudinem, quam perpetua in omni vita cogitatio, nihil esse quod accidere non possit : quam meditatio conditionis humanæ, quam vitæ lex, commentatioque parendi : quæ non hoc affert, ut semper mœreamus sed ut nunquam. *Id.* [*III*, 16].

Ergo is, quisquis est, qui moderatione, et constantia quietus animo est, sibique ipse placatus, ut neque tabescat molestiis, neque frangatur, timore, nec sitienter quid appetens ardeat desiderio, nec alacritate furtili gestiens deliquescat : is est sapiens, quem quaerimus : is est beatus, cui nihil humanarum rerum aut intolerabile ad demittendum animum, aut nimis lætabile ad efferendum videre potest. *Id. Lib.* 4. [17]

[LIVY] (1)

His ego gratiora dictu alia esse scio : sed me vera pro gratis loqui, etsi meum ingenium non moneret, necessitas cogit. Vellem equidem vobis placere, Quirites ; sed multo vos salvos esse, qualicumque erga me animo futuri estis.

Orat. T. Quincti Capitolihi ad populum Rom. Lib. Liv. 3. *cap.* 68.

(1) Different and probably later handwriting.

Diodorus declares that only will happen which is either
true or will be true : and whatever will be true, he says,
must necessarily happen ; and whatever will not be true,
according to him may not happen.

Doubtful, not impious, I lived
Uncertain I die, not perturbed.
It is human to ignore and to err.
Being of beings have mercy on me.

We follow our fate here and there wherever it takes us.
Whatever will happen, destiny must be ovecome, by
bearing it.

Time wastes too fast ! Every letter I trace tells me with what rapidity life follows my pen. The days and hours of it are flying over our heads like clouds of a winday never to return more ! Everything presses on : and every time I kiss thy hand to bid adieu, every absence which follows it, are preludes to that eternal separation which we are shortly to make !

Sterne.

Diodorus id solum fieri posse dicit, quod aut sit verum aut futurum sit verum : et, quidquid futurum sit, id dicit fieri necesse est ; et quidquid non sit futurum, id negat fieri posse (1).

Cicero, de fato, c. 7.

Dubius non impius vixi
Incertus morior, non perturbatus.
Humanum est nescire et errare.
Ens entium miserere mei.

D. *of Buckingham epitaph.*

..... quo fata trahunt, retrahuntque, sequamur.
Quicquid erit, superanda omnis fortuna ferendo est.

[Virgil's AE, V, 709].

(1) Also found in *The Commonplace Book*, art. 865, but without attribution to any author.

EURIPIDES

Ungrateful is your race, you who are zealous for an orator's honors ; may you be unknown to me, you who care not if you hurt your friend, provided you say something that pleases the multitude.

Rulers should not use their power wrongly nor when enjoying good fortune expect always to be prosperous.

A word coming from men of no standing and the same word from men of position have not the same force.

In this are most cities harmed whenever a man who is noble and zealous wins no higher prize than baser men.

Nay for myself while living day by day, even if my lot were humble, it would be quite enough ; but as for a tomb I should wish mine to be one that men, seeing, honor ; long enduring is that satisfaction.

EURIPIDES

'Αχάριστον ὑμῶν σπέρμ᾽, δημηγόρους
ζηλοῦτε τιμάς, μηδέ γιγνώςκοισθέ μοι,
"Οι τοὺς φίλους βλάπτοντες, οὐ φροντίζετε.
"Ην τοῖσι πολλοῖς πρὸς χάριν λέγητέ τι.

Hecuba. v. 254.

Οὐ τοὺς κρατοῦντας χρὴ κρατεῖν ἃ μὴ χρέων.
Οὐδ᾽ εὐτυχοῦντας, εὖ δοκεῖν πράζειν ἀεί.

Id. v. 282.

— Λόγος γὰρ ἔκ τ᾽ ἀδοξούντων ἰὼν,
κᾀκ τῶν δοκούντων αὐτὸς, οὐ ταύτον σθένει.

Id. v. 294.

'Εν τῷδε γάρ κάμνουσιν αἱ πολλαὶ πόλεις,
"Οταν τις ἐσθλὸς καὶ πρόθυμος ὢν ἀνήρ,
μηδὲν φέρηται τῶν κακιόνων πλέον.

Id. v. 306.

Καὶ μην ἔμοιγε ζῶντι μὲν καθ᾽ ἡμέραν,
κ᾽ εἰ σμίκρ᾽ ἔχοιμι ,πάντ᾽ ἂν ἀκρούντως ἔχοι ·
τύμβον δὲ βουλοίμην ἂν ἀξιούμενον
τὸν ἐμὸν ὁρᾶσθαι · διὰ μακροῦ γάρ ἡ χάρις.

Id. v. 317.

He who is not wont to taste of ills bears them, but grieves when he has set his neck beneath the yoke. Dying he would be much happier than living, for to live ignoble is a great burden. To be of the noble born gives a peculiar distinction clearly marked among men, and the noble name increases in lustre in those who are worthy.

Strange if bad soil, obtaining good season from Providence, bears a rich harvest, while good soil, lacking what it must have, gives evil fruit. Among men he who is evil is never aught but base, and the noble man is noble, neither through circumstance does he mar his nature but is ever upright. Would you say parents or nurture make the difference ? To be sure an excellent training teaches nobleness ; if a man learns this well he also knows what baseness is, since he by the standard of honor he learns it.

Ὅς τις γὰρ οὐκ εἴωθε γεύεσθαι κακῶν,
φέρει μέν, ἀλγεῖ δ'αὐχέν' ἐντιθεὶς ζυγῷ.
θανών δ' ἂν εἴη μᾶλλον εὐτυχέστερος,
ἢ ζῶν. Τό γὰρ Ζῆν μὴ καλῶς μέγας πόνος.
Δεινὸς χαρακτήρ, κἀπίσημος ἐν βροτοῖς.
ἐσθλῶν γενέσθαι. κἀπὶ μεῖζον ἔρχεται
τῆς εὐγενείας τοὔνομα τοῖσιν ἀξίοις

Id. v. 375.

— Οὔκουν δεινόν, εἰ γῆ μὲν κακὴ.
Τυχοῦσα καιροῦ θεόθεν, εὖ στάχυν φέρει,
χρηστὴ δ' ἁμαρτοῦς' ὧν χρεὼν αὐτὴν τυχεῖν,
κακόν δίδωσι καρπόν. ἄνθρωποι δ'ἀεὶ
ὁ μὲν πονηρὸς, οὐδὲν ἄλλο πλὴν κακός.
ὁ δ'ἐσθλὸς, ἐσθλός. οὐδὲ συμφορᾶς ὕπο
φύσιν διέφθειρ' ἀλλά χρηστός ἐστ' δ'ἀεὶ ·
ἆρ οἱ τεκόντες διαφέρουσιν, ἢ τροφαί ;
ἔχει γε μεν τοί τι καὶ τὸ θρεφθῆναι καλῶς,
δίδαξιν ἐσθλοῦ. τοῦτ' δέ ἤν τις εὖ μάθη,
οἶδεν τό γ' αἰσχρόν, κανόνι τοῦ καλοῦ μαθών.

Id. v. 593.

                        He is most happy
To whom day after day no ill befalls.

The good man's task is to serve the right and everywhere,
to treat harshly evil-doers.

Alas, no one among mortals is free ; for either he is
the slave of wealth or fortune, or else the populace or legal
technicalities compel him to resort to practices that are
contrary to his belief.

Alas, there is nothing we may trust, nor is there honor,
nor any assurance that faring well we shall not fare ill.
But the gods mingle things confusedly, introducing disorder,
that we may worship them in ignorance.

Liability to human law and to the gods, wherever it
coincides.

— Κεῖνος ὀλβιώτατος,
ὅτῳ κατ᾽ ἦμαρ τυγχάνει μηδὲν κακόν.

Id. v. 627.

ἐσθλοῦ γὰρ ἀνδρὸς τῇ δίκῃ θ᾽ ὑπερετεῖν,
καὶ τοὺς κακοὺς δρᾶν πανταχοῦ κακῶς ἀεί.

Id. v. 844.

Φεῦ, οὐκ ἔστι θνητῶν ὅςτις ἔστ᾽ ἐλεύθερος.
ἢ χρημάτων γὰρ δοῦλός ἐστιν, ἢ τύχης,
ἢ πλῆθος αὐτὸν πόλεος, ἢ νόμων γραφαὶ
εἴργουσι χρῆσθαι μὴ κατὰ γνώμην τρόποις.

Id. v. 864.

Φεῦ, οὐκ ἔστιν οὐδὲν πιστὸν, οὔτ᾽ εὐδοξία,
οὔτ᾽ αὖ καλῶς πράσσοντα, μὴ πράξειν κακῶς.
φύρουσι δ᾽ αὔθ᾽ οἱ θεοὶ πάλιν τε καὶ πρόσω,
ταραγμὸν ἐντιθέντες, ὡς ἀγνωσίᾳ
σέβωμεν αὐτούς.

Id. v. 956.

Τὸ γὰρ ὑπέγγυον
·δίκᾳ καὶ θεοῖς, οὐ ξυμπιτνεῖ.

Id. v. 1029.

To the doer of infamous deeds God awards a fearful penalty.

Among men never should speech be stronger than deeds, but if they are doers of good deed nobly should they speak, and if their deeds are evil their words should be unsound, and never should they be able to speak persuasively things that are unjust. Crafty are they who have cultivated these things but not forever can they remain crafty; foully they perish, never has any escaped.

Harsh is necessity.

There is nothing so fearful to tell, no calamity or misfortune sent by the gods, the weight of which man's nature might not bear.

O sovereign oblivion of suffering, how wise thou art and to the unhappy a god to be invoked with prayers.

Δράσαντι δ'αἰσχρὰ, δεινὰ τἀπιτίμια
δαίμων δέδωκεν ·

Id. v. 1086.

— ἀνθρώποισιν οὐκ ἐχρῆν ποτέ
τῶν πραγμάτων τὴν γλῶσσαν ἰσχύειν πλέον.
ἀλλ' εἴτε χρήστ' ἔδρασι, χρήστ' ἔδει λέγειν ·
εἶτ' αὖ πονηρά, τοὺς λόγους εἶναι σαθρούς,
καὶ μὴ δύνασθαι τἄδικ' εὐλλέγειν ποτέ.
σοφοὶ μὲν οὖν εἰσ' οἱ τἄδ' ἠκριβωκότες,
ἀλλ' οὐ δύναινται διά τέλους εἶναι σοφοί,
κακῶς δ'ἀπώλοντο, κού τις ἐξηλυξέ πω.

Id. v. 1187.

— Στερρὰ γὰρ ἀνάγκη.

Id. v. 1293.

Οὐκ ἔστιν οὐδὲν δεινὸν, ὧδ' εἰπεῖν ἔπος,
οὐδὲ πάθος, οὐδὲ ξυμφορὰ θεήλατος,
ἧς οὐκ ἂν ἄραιτ' ἄχθος ἀνθρώπου φύσις.

Orestes v. 1.

Ὦ πότνια λήθη τῶν κακῶν, ὡς εἶ σοφὴ
καὶ τοῖσι δυστυχοῦσιν εὐκταία θεός.

[*Id. v.* 210].

Change in all things is sweet.

Such acts of helpfulness are, in the eyes of friends, beautiful.

Great happiness is not lasting among men, but Providence as though smiting the sail of a swift vessel, submerges it in fearful troubles as within furious, destructful, waves of the sea.

They are friends in name, not in reality who are not friends in misfortunes.

Enviable is he who has been fortunate in his children and has not brought upon himself notable misfortunes.

Happy is the life of those whose marriages have come to a good issue, but those to whom they fall out ill both at home and abroad are unfortunate.

— Μεταβολὴ πάντων γλυκύ,

Id. v. 324.

Ἐπικουρίαι γὰρ αἵδε τοῖς φίλοις καλαί.

Id. 300.

ὁ μέγας ὄλϐος οὐ μόνιμος ἐν βροτοῖς.
ἀνὰ δὲ λαῖφος ὥς τις ἀκάτου θοᾶς
τινάξας δαίμων, κατέκλυσε,
δεινῶν πόνων, ὡς πόντου,
λάϐροις ὀλεθρίοισιν ἐν κύμασι.

Id. v. 340.

Ὄνομα γάρ, ἔργον δ' οὐκ ἔχουσιν οἱ φίλοι
οἱ μὴ 'πὶ ταῖσι συμφοραῖς ὄντες φίλοι

Id. v. 454.

Ζηλωτὸς, ὅστις εὐτύχησεν εἰς τέκνα,
καὶ μὴ 'πισήμους συμφορὰς ἐκτήσαντο.

Id. v. 541.

Γάμοι δ' ὅσοις μὲν εὐκαθεστᾶσι Βροτῶν,
μακάριος αἰών · οἷς δὲ μὴ πίπτουσιν εὖ
τά τ' ἔνδον εἰσὶ, τά τε θύραζε δυστυχεῖς

Id. v. 601.

There are times when silence would be better than speech, there are times when speech would be preferable to silence.

In troubles we should help friends, but when Fortune is generous what need is there of friends ?   Providence alone is enough, if she wishes to help.

For with slight efforts how should one obtain great results ?   It is foolish even to desire it.

A man faithful amid adversities is fairer to behold than calm to mariners.

How, being a friend, shall I show I am one unless I help you when you are in fearful misfortunes ?

Whenever a man winning in words but evil in thoughts persuades the multitude, a great evil it is for the city. But they who with understanding counsel ever good things, if not at once later are of help to the city.

— Ἔστι δ'οὗ σιγὴ λόγου ·
κρείσσων γένοιτ'ἄν. ἔστι δ'οὗ σιγῆς λόγος.

Id. v. 637.

Ἐν τοῖς κακοῖς χρὴ τοῖς φίλοισιν ὠφελεῖν.
Ὅταν δ'ὁ δαίμων εὖ διδῷ, τί χρὴ φίλων;
Ἀρκεῖ γὰρ αὐτὸς ὁ θεός, ὠφελεῖν θέλων.

Id. v. 665.

Σμικροῖσι γὰρ τὰ μεγάλα πῶς ἕλοι τις ἂν
πόνοισιν; ἀμαθὲς καὶ τὸ βούλεσθαι τάδε.

Id. v. 694.

— Πιστὸς ἐν κακοῖς ἀνήρ,
κρείσσων γαλήνης ναυτίλοισιν εἰσορᾶν.

Id. v. 725.

Ποῦ γὰρ ὢν δείξω φίλος,
εἴ σε μὴ ἐν δειναῖσιν ὄντα συμφοραῖς ἐπαρκέσω —

Id. v. 800.

Ὅταν γὰρ ἡδὺς τοῖς λόγοις, φρονῶν κακῶς,
πείθῃ τὸ πλῆθος, τῇ πόλει κακὸν μέγα.
ὅσοι δὲ σὺν νῷ χρηστὰ βουλεύουσ' ἀεί,
κἂν μὴ παραυτίκ', αὖθις εἰσι χρήσιμοι.
πόλει.

Id. v. 907.

Alas, alas, races of mortals, wholly inspiring tears, much lamenting and much toiling ! Behold how contrary to expectation fate goes her way ! Now to one, now to another, and to each in turn she metes troubles after a long season, and all the life of men is unstable.

Nothing is better than a reliable friend, not riches, not absolute sovereignty. Nay more, the crowd is not to be reckoned with, in exchange for a noble friend.

God sets an end for men, an end that lied where he wills.

Scandal-loving is womankind by nature, and if they find slight pretexts for fables, then inventing greater ones. Some sort of leasure there is for woman to tell one another things unsound.

Money by men is esteemed above all else, and of the things among men it has the greatest power.

Ἰὼ, ἰώ, πανδάκρυτ᾽ ἐφαμέρων ἔθνη
πολύσονα τε δὴ καὶ πολύπονα, λεύσσεθ᾽ ὡς παρ᾽ ἐλπίδα.
μοῖρα βαίνει
ἕτερα δ᾽ἑτέροις ἀμείϐεται
πήματ᾽ ἐν χρόνῳ μακρῷ,
βροτῶν δ᾽ὁ πᾶς ἀστάθμητος αἰών.

Id. v. 974.

— Οὐκ ἔστιν οὐδὲν κρεῖσσον, ἢ φίλος σαφής
οὐ πλοῦτος, οὐ τυραννίς. ἀλόγιστον δέ τι
τὸ πλῆθος, ἀντάλλαγμα γενναίου φίλου.

Id. 1155.

Τέλος ἔχει δαίμων βροτοῖσι, τέλος ὅπᾳ θέλει.

Id. v. 1545.

Φιλόψογον γὰρ χρῆμα θηλειῶν ἔφυ,
σμικρὰς δ᾽ ἀφορμὰς ἢν λάϐωσι τῶν λόγων,
πλείους ἐπεισφέρουσιν. ἡδονὴ δέ τις
γυναιξὶ, μηδὲν ὑγιὲς ἀλλήλαις λέγειν.

Phœnissæ v. 206.

Τὰ χρήματ᾽ ἀνθρώποισι τιμιώτατα,
Δύναμίν τε πλείστην τῶν ἐν ἀνθρώποις ἔχει.

[*Id. v.* 439].

Plain is the word of truth, and of elaborate interpretations justice has no need ; of herself she is fitting. But the unrighteous word, being unsound, needs cunning allurements.

We must not speak highly of ignoble actions, for this is not a noble thing but on the contrary bitter to justice.

Experience has something wiser to tell than youth.

This is better... to honor equality, which ever unites friends to friends, cities to cities, allies to allies. For equality is in accord with the laws of men. But to the greater ever stands opposed the lesser, and it brings on days of hatred.

What is gain ? It exists but in name, since enough is sufficient to the wise. Not as their own do mortals hold their possessions but we are stewards of gifts we receive from the gods. When they crave them they take them back again. Wealth is not stable, it lasts but a day.

Ἁπλοῦς ὁ μῦθος τῆς ἀληθείας ἔφυ,
κοὺ ποικίλων δεῖ τὰ 'νδιχ' ἑρμηνευμάτων,
ἔχει γὰρ αὐτὰ καιρόν · ὁ δ' ἄδικος λόγος
νοσῶν ἐν αὑτῷ, φαρμάκων δεῖται σοφῶν

Id. v. 472.

Οὐκ εὖ λέγειν χρὴ μὴ 'πὶ τοῖς ἔργοις καλοῖς
οὐ γὰρ καλὸν τοῦτ', ἀλλὰ τῇ δίκῃ πικρόν.

Id. v. 529.

— ἡ 'μπειρία
ἔχει τι λέξαι τῶν νέων σοφώτερον

Id. v. 532.

— Κεῖνο κάλλιον, —
'ισότητα τιμᾶν · ἢ φίλους ἀεὶ φίλοις,
πόλεις τε πόλεσι, ξυμμάχους τε ξυμμάχοις
συνδεῖ · τὸ γὰρ ἴσον, νόμιμον ἀνθρώποις ἔφυ.
τῷ πλέονι δ' αἰεὶ πολέμιον καθίσταται.
τοὔλασσον, ,ἐχθρᾶς θ' ἡμέρας κατάρχεται

Id. v. 538.

— τί δ' ἔστι τὸ πλέον ; ὄνομ' ἔχει μόνον.
ἐπεὶ τἄγ' ἀκροῦνθ' ἑκανὰ τοῖσι σώφροσιν.
Οὔτοι τὰ χρήματ, ἴδια κέκτηνται βροτοί.
τὰ τῶν Θεῶν δ' ἔχοντες ἐπιμελούμεθα.
ὅταν δὲ χρῄζως' αὐτὰ 'φαιροῦνται πάλιν.
ὁ δ' ὄλβος οὐ βέβαιος, ἀλλ' ἐφήμερος.

Id. v. 558.

All things are easy for the gods.

For if each man taking up something serviceable as best he may should go through with it and contribute it to his country, nations should experience lesser evils in the future and prosper.

If servants are good, when the fortunes of their master take an evil turn, they still are touched.

Each man loves himself better than his neighbor.

To be accustomed to live on the common level is better : be it mine, if not in greatness, at least in peace to grow old.

Πάντα δ'εὐπετῆ θεοῖς.

Id. v. 696.

εἰ γὰρ λαβὼν ἕκαστος ὅ τι δύναιτό τις
χρηστὸν, διέλθοι τοῦτο, κεἰς κοινὸν φέροι
πατρίδι, κακῶν ἂν αἱ πόλεις ἐλασσόνων
πειρώμεναι, τὸ λοιπὸν εὐτυχοῖεν ἄν.

Id. v. 1022.

Χρηστοῖσι δούλοις ξυμφορὰ τὰ δεσποτῶν
κακῶς πίτνοντα, καὶ φρενῶν ἀνθάπτεται.

Medæa. v. 54.

— πᾶς τις αὐτὸν τοῦ πέλας μᾶλλον φιλεῖ.

Id. v. 86.

Τὸ γὰρ εἰθίσθαι ζῆν ἐπ' ἴσοισι,
κρεῖσσον · ἔμοι γ' οὖν, εἰ μὴ μεγαλως,
ὀχυρῶς τ' εἴη καταγηράσκειν.

[Id. 122].

If you bring new wisdom to dullards, you will seem
to be profitless, not wise.

O Zeus, why hast thou given a clear test of gold that
is brass, whereas there is not token on the body by which
one may distinguish the evil man.

His every friend flees from the path of a poor man.

Mortals should beget children from some other source
and there should be no womankind ; thus there would be
no ill for men.

Thankless may he perish, who cannot honor his friends,
opening up the unsullied lock of his heart ; to me he shall
never be a friend.

Gold is more precious than countless words to men.

With a light heart must we bear misfortunes, since we
are men.

Not for the first time now do I esteem mortality a
shadow.

Σκαιοῖσι μὲν γὰρ καινὰ προσφέρων σοφὰ
δόξεις ἀχρεῖος. κοὐ σοφὸς πεφυκέναι.

Id. v. 298.

Ὦ Ζεῦ, τί δὴ χρυσοῦ μὲν ὃς κίβδηλος ἦ,
τεκμήρι᾽ ἀνθρώποισιν ὤπασας σαφῆ,
ἀνδρῶν δ᾽ ὅτῳ χρὴ τὸν κακὸν διειδέναι,
οὐδεὶς χαρακτὴρ ἐμπέφυκε σώματι.

Id. v. 516.

Πένητα φεύγει πᾶς τις ἐκποδὼν φίλος.

Id. v. 561.

— χρῆν γὰρ ἄλλοθέν ποθεν βροτοὺς
παῖδας τεκνοῦσθαι, θῆλυ δ᾽ οὐκ εἶναι γένος.
οὕτως δ᾽ ἂν οὐκ ἦν οὐδὲν ἀνθρώποις κακὸν ·

Id. v. 573.

Ἀχάριστος ὄλοιθ᾽, ὅτῳ πάρεσται
μὴ φίλους τιμᾷν, καθαρὰν ἀνοίξαν —
τι κλῆιδα φρενῶν ·
κἀμοὶ φίλος οὔ ποτ᾽ ἔσται .

Id. v. 659.

Χρυσὸς δὴ κρείσσων μυρίων λόγων βροτοῖς

[*Id. v.* 965.]

κούφως φέρειν χρὴ θνητὸν ὄντα συμφοράς.

Id. v. 1018.

Τὰ θνητὰ δ᾽ οὐ νῦν πρῶτον ἡγοῦμαι σκιάν.

Id. v. 1224.

No man among mortals is happy.   With fortune streaming towards him one man may be more lucky than another, but happy ?   No.

Master of many things is Zeus in Olympus, and many things contrary to expectation the gods accomplish. Things expected are not fulfilled and for things unexpected Providence finds a way.

You must forgive if one whose heart through youth is violent speaks thoughtlessly.   Do not appear to hear him.

The whole life of man is grievous and there is no rest from troubles, but whatever it be that is better than life. Embracing darkness hides in the clouds.   Therefore, madly infatuated we appear with this light that glitters upon earth through want of experience of another life and for lack of revelation of the under world.

More easily shalt thou bear thy sickness with quietness and a noble courage ; to suffer is man's fate.

The good we understand and we know, but we don't carry it to fulfilment, some from laziness, some preferring some pleasure or other to the noble.   Pleasures are many in life, long gossippings, and idleness, a pleasant evil, and sense of shame...

Moderation everywhere is beautiful and assures good repute among men.

θνητῶν γὰρ οὐδείς ἐστιν εὐδαίμων ἀνήρ.
ὄλβου δ᾽ἐπιρρυέντος, εὐτυχέστερος
ἄλλου γένοιτ᾽ ἂν ἄλλος, εὐδαίμων δ᾽ἂν οὔ.

                                    Id. v. 1228.

Πολλῶν ταμίας Ζεὺς ἐν ὀλύμπῳ,
πολλὰ δ᾽ἀέλπτως κραίνουσι θεοί.
καὶ τὰ δοκηθέντ᾽ οὐκ ἐτελέσθη,
τῶν δ᾽ἀδοκήτων πόρον εὗρε θεός.

                                    Id. v. 1415.

— Χρὴ δὲ συγγνώμην ἔχειν,
εἴ τίς γ᾽ ὑφ᾽ ἥβης σπλάγχνον ἔντονον φέρων,
μάταια βάζει · μὴ δόκει τούτου κλύειν.

                                Hippolytus. v. 117.

Πᾶς δ᾽ ὀδυνηρὸς βίος ἀνθρώπων,
κοὐκ ἔστι πόνων ἀνάπαυσις ·
ἀλλ᾽ ὅ, τι τοῦ ζῆν φίλτερον ἄλλο,
σκότος ἀμπίσχον κρύπτει νεφέλαις.
δυσέρωτες δὴ φαινόμεθ᾽ ὄντες
τοῦδ᾽ ὅτι τοῦτο στίλβει κατὰ γῆν
δι᾽ ἀπειροσύναν ἄλλου βιότου,
κοὐκ ἀπόδειξιν τῶν ὑπὸ γαίας.

                                    Id. v. 189.

Ῥᾷον δὲ νόσον μετὰ θ᾽ ἡσυχίας
καὶ γενναίου λήματος οἴσεις ·
μοχθεῖν δὲ βροτοῖσιν, ἀνάγκη.

                                    Id. v. 205.

Τὰ χρήστ᾽ ἐπιστάμεσθα, καὶ γιγνώσκομεν,
οὐκ ἐκπονοῦμεν δ᾽. οἱ μὲν ἀργίας ὕπο,
οἱ δ᾽ ἡδονὴν προθέντες ἀντὶ τοῦ καλοῦ
ἄλλην τιν᾽. εἰσὶ δ᾽ἡδοναὶ πολλαὶ βίου,
μακραί τε λέσχαι, καὶ σχολὴ τερπνὸν κακόν,
αἰδώς τε. —

                                    Id. v. 380.

— τὸ σῶφρον ὡς ἀπανταχοῦ καλὸν.
καὶ δόξαν ἐσθλὴν ἐν βροτοῖς κομίζεται

                                    Id. v. 431.

.....In   mortals
second thoughts are somehow wiser.

Dare if thou love ; a god has willed this.   If thou art
ailing, subdue thoroughly thine ailment.

O Zeus, why hast thou established women, a curse
deceiving men, in the light of the sun ?   If thou didst
wish to beget a race of men, not from women should it be
necessary to procure them, but men by placing in temples
bronze, or iron, or a weight of gold in exchange should
buy seed of children, each in proportion to the value of
his offering and then live in carefree homes, far from
women. But now when we are about to bring this curse
into our homes, we pay our household wealth as a penalty.
But this it is clear how great a curse woman is : adding
a dower the father who begat and reared her sends her
away from home that he may be rid of his curse.

But he who takes into his home a curse, working harm,
rejoices, putting fair adorments on the most ugly image,
and sets it off with robes, unfortunate man, in secret
driving happiness from his home.   He has no choice but
either, allied by marriage with noble kinsfolk, content
he maintains the bitter union or, gaining a good wife
but fruitless kin, he forces down his ill luck with the good.
His lot is most easy who has a nobody...

. . . . . . κἀν βροτοῖς
ἁι δεύτεραί πως φροντίδες σοφώτεραι.

Id. v. 435.

Τόλμα δ'ἐρῶσα · θεὸς ἐβουλήθη τάδε.
νοσοῦσα δ'εὖ πῶς τὴν νόσον καταστρέφου.

Id. v. 476.

ᵓΩ Ζεῦ, τί δὴ κίβδηλον ἀνθρώποις κακὸν,
γυναῖκας, εἰς φῶς ἡλίου κατῴκισας ;
εἰ γὰρ βρότειον ἤθελες σπεῖραι γένος,
οὐκ ἐκ γυναικῶν χρῆν παραχέσθαι τόδε.
ἀλλ' ἀντιθέντας σοῖσιν ἐν ναοῖς βροτοὺς
ἢ χαλκὸν, ἢ σίδηρον, ἢ χρυσοῦ βάρος,
παίδων πρίασθαι σπέρμα, τοῦ τιμήματος
τῆς ἀξίας ἕκαστον · ἐν δὲ δώμασι
ναίειν ἐλευθέροισι, θηλειῶν ἄτερ.
νῦν δ' ᾽ εἰς δόμους μὲν πρῶτον ἄξεσθαι κακὸν
μέλλοντες, ὄλβον δωμάτων ἐκτίνομεν.
τούτῳ δὲ δῆλον, ὡς γυνὴ κακὸν μέγα ·
προσθεὶς γὰρ ὁ σπείρας τε καὶ θρέψας πατὴρ
φερνὰς, ἀπῴκισ', ὡς ἀπαλλαχθῇ κακοῦ.
ὁ δ' αὖ λαβὼν ἀτηρὸν εἰς δόμους κακὸν,
γέγηθε, κόσμον προστιθεὶς ἀγάλματι
καλὸν κακίστῳ, καὶ πέπλοισιν ἐκπονεῖ,
δύστηνος, ὄλβον δωμάτων ὑπεξελών.
ἔχει δ'ἀνάγκην, ὥστε κηδεύσας καλοῖς
γαμβροῖσι, χαίρων σῴζεται πικρὸν λέχος ·
ἢ χρηστὰ λέκτρα, πενθερούς δ'ἀνωφελεῖς
λαβὼν, πιέζει τἀγαθῷ τὸ δυστυχές.
ῥᾷστον δ'ὅτῳ τὸ μηδέν,

Id. v. 616.

Mayest thou perish and whosoever is zealous not to do good service nobly to unwilling friends.

Our lot determines our thoughts.

Alas, there should be established for mortals some sure test of their friends and some token of their hearts, to show who is true and who is not a friend, and all men should have two voices, the one honest, the other as it might chance to be, that the unjust voice might be exposed by the just and we not be deceived.

Alas for the heart of man. How far will it go ? What limit shall there be for insolence and presumption ? For if it go on swelling from generation to generation this latter age be more unscrupulous than the former, the gods will need to add a new earth to this, that will hold the unjust and those who by nature are evil.

Ὄλοιο καὶ σὺ, χ' ὥστις ἄκοντας φίλους
πρόθυμος ἐστι μὴ καλῶς εὐεργετεῖν

Id. v. 693.

Πρὸς τὰς τύχας γὰρ τὰς φρένας κεκτήμεθα.

Id. v. 701.

Φεῦ, χρῆν βροτοῖσι τῶν φίλων τεκμήριον
σαφές τι κεῖσθαι, καὶ διάγνωσιν φρενῶν.
ὅστις τ' ἀληθής ἐστιν, ὅς τε μὴ φίλος ·
δισσὰς δὲ φωνὰς πάντας ἀνθρώπους ἔχειν,
Τὴν μὲν δικαίαν, τὴν δ' ὅπως ἐτύγχανεν.
ὡς ἡ φρονοῦσα τἄδικ' ἐξηλέγχετο
πρὸς τῆς δικαίας, κοὐκ ἂν ἠπατώμεθα.

Id. v. 925.

Φεῦ, τῆς βροτείας ποῖ προβήσεται φρενός ;
τί τέρμα τόλμης καὶ θράσους γενήσεται ;
εἰ γὰρ κατ'ἀνδρὸς βίοτον ἐξογκώσεται,
ὁδ' ὕστερος τοῦ πρόσθεν εἰς ὑπερβολὴν
πανοῦργος ἔσται, θεοῖσι προσβαλεῖν χθονὶ
ἄλλην δεήσει γαῖαν, ἢ χωρήσεται
τοὺς μὴ δικαίους καὶ κακοὺς πεφυκότας.

Id. v. 936.

Those who among the wise are of no account are to the crowd rather accomplished in speech.

A sudden death is easiest to an unfortunate man.

At the death of the righteous the gods do not rejoice. The wicked, with their children and homes, we destroy.

.....For men to sin is reasonable, when gods offer the occasion.

— Οἱ γὰρ ἐν σοφοῖς
φαῦλοι, παρ' ὄχλῳ μουσικώτεροι λέγειν.

Id. v. 988.

Ταχὺς γὰρ ᾅδης ῥᾷστος ἀνδρὶ δυστυχεῖ

Id. v. 1047.

— Τοὺς γὰρ εὐσεβεῖς Θεοὶ
θνῄσκοντας οὐ χαίρουσι · τούς γε μὴν κακοὺς
αὐτοῖς τέκνοισι καὶ δόμοις ἐξόλλυμεν.

Id. v. 1338.

— Ἀνθρώποισι δὲ,
θεῶν διδόντων, εἰκὸς ἐξαμαρτάνειν

Id. v. 1433.

HOMER'S ILIAD

Cattle and goodly sheep may be won as booty and tripods and yellow-maned horses may be acquired but the soul of man may not be caught or seized to come back again when once it shall pass the ridge-fence of the teeth.

Thus forsooth upon us from birth Zeus sends a grievous woe.

O brother, if we were to escape from this war and be ageless and deathless forever, never would I fight among the foremost nor would I send thee into men-ennobling battles. But now, since unnumbered deadly fates stand about us which men may not shun nor avoid let us go forward.

HOMERS' ILIAD

Ληϊστοὶ μὲν γάρ τε βόες καὶ ἴφια μῆλα,
Κτητοὶ δὲ τρίποδές τε, καὶ ἵππων ξανθὰ κάρηνα ·
Ἀνδρὸς δὲ ψυχὴ πάλιν ἐλθεῖν οὔτε λεϊστὴ,
οὔθ᾽ ἑλετή, ἐπεὶ ἄρ κεν ἀμείψεται ἕρκος ὀδόντων.

Il. I. v. 406.

— ὧδε που ἄμμι
Ζεὺς ἐπιγιγνομένοισιν ἵει κακότητα βαρεῖαν

Il. K. v. 70.

Ὦ πέπον, εἰ μὲν γὰρ πόλεμον περὶ τόνδε φυγόντε,
αἰεὶ δὴ μέλλοιμεν ἀγήρω τ᾽ ἀθανάτω τε
ἔσσεσθ᾽, οὔτε κεν αὐτὸς ἐνὶ πρώτοισι μαχοίμην,
οὔτέ κε σὲ στέλλοιμι μάχην ἐς κυδιάνειραν ·
Νῦν δε ἔμπης γὰρ κῆρες ἐφεστᾶσιν θανάτοιο
μυρίαι, ἃς οὐκ ἔστι φυγεῖν βροτὸν, οὐδ᾽ὑπαλύξαι,
ἴομεν —

Il. M. v. 322.

For there is nothing more pitiable than man, of all creatures that breathe and crawl upon the earth.

Pliant is the tongue of man and it possesses many and diverse words, and wide is the range of speech hither and thither.

For there is not profit in chilling lament, since thus the gods have spun the fate of wretched mortals, to live in misery, while they themselves are free from care. Two jars stand on the floor of Zeus' palace, holding gifts which he gives — evil the one, and good the other. To whomsoever Zeus who delights in thunder gives a gift, intermingling from both, such a man encounters now evil and now good. But the man to whom he gives from his gifts of bale he has marked with dishonor, and him vile grinding misery drives over the wondrous earth ; he wanders, honored neither by gods nor by men.

Οὐ μὲν γάρ τί πού ἐστὶν οἰζυρώτερον ἀνδρὸς
παντῶν, ὅσσα τε γαῖαν ἐπι πνείει τε καὶ ἕρπει

Il. P. v. 446.

Στρεπτὴ τὲ γλῶσσ' ἐστὶ βροτῶν, πολέες δ'ἔνι μῦθοι
παντοῖοι, ἐπέων δὲ πολὺς νομὸς ἔνθα καὶ ἔνθα.

Il. Υ. 248.

οὐ γάρ τις πρῆξις πέλεται κρυεροῖο γόοιο.
ὣς γὰρ ἐπεκλώσαντο θεοὶ δειλοῖσι βροτοῖσι,
ζώειν ἀχνυμένους · αὐτοὶ δέ τ'ἀκηδέες εἰσί.
δοιοὶ γάρ τε πίθοι κατακείαται ἐν Διὸς οὔδει
δώρον, οἶα δίδωσι, κακῶν, ἕτερος δὲ ἑάων.
ᾧ μὲν κ' ἀμμίξας δώῃ Ζεὺς τερπικέραυνος,
ἄλλοτε μέν τε κακῷ ὅ γε κύρεται, ἄλλοτε δ'ἐσθλῷ.
ᾧ δέ κε τῶν λυγρῶν δώῃ, λωβητὸν ἔθηκε.
καί ἑ κακὴ βούβρωστις ἐπὶ χθόνα δῖαν ἐλαύνει,
φοιτᾷ δ'οὔτε θεοῖσι τετιμένος οὔτε βροτοῖσιν.

Il. Ω. 524.

HOMER'S ODYSSEY.

Straightway he cast a drug into the wine of which they were drinking, a drug free from pain and bitterness, causing forgetfulness of all evils. And whoever should swallow it down, when it was mixed in the mixing bowl no longer day after day would shed tears down his cheeks, not even if before him they slew his brother or his own son and he with his own eyes beheld it.

Nothing more feeble than man does earth nourish, of all creatures that breathe and crawl upon the earth. Never hereafter he says shall he suffer evil, so long as the gods grant him prowess and his limbs have power to move. But when the blessed gods bring bitter things to pass, these also he bears, though unwilling, with a patient heart. For the mood of mortal men is such as day by day the father of gods and men induces.

HOMER'S ODYSSEY.

αὐτίκ᾽ ἄρ᾽ εἰς οἶνον βάλε φάρμακον, ἔνθεν ἔπινον,
νυπενθές τ᾽ ἄχολόν τε, κακῶν ἐπίληθον ἁπάντων.
ὃς τὸ καταβρόξειεν, ἐπὴν, κρητῆρι μιγείη,
οὔ κεν ἐφημέριός γε βάλοι κατὰ δάκρυ παρειῶν,
οὐδ᾽ εἴ οἱ προπάροιθεν ἀδελφεὸν ἢ φίλον υἱὸν
χαλκῷ δηιόωεν, ὁ δ᾽ ὀφθαλμοῖσιν ὁρῷτο.

Od. Δ. 220.

οὐδὲν ἀκιδνότερον γαῖα τρέφει ἀνθρώποιο
πάντων, ὅσσα τε γαῖαν ἔπι πνείεν τε καὶ ἕρπει
οὐ μὲν γάρ ποτέ φησί κακὸν πείσεσθαι ὀπίσσω,
ὄφρ᾽ ἀρετὴν παρέχωσι θεοὶ καὶ γούνατ᾽ ὀρώρῃ
ἀλλ᾽ ὅτε δὴ καὶ λυγρὰ θεοὶ μάκαρες τελέσωσι,
καὶ τὰ τφέφει ἀεκαζόμενος τετληότε θύμῳ ·
τοῖος γὰρ νόος ἐστὶν ἐπιχθονίων ἀνθρώπων,
οἷον ἐπ᾽ ἦμαρ ἄγησι πατὴρ ἀνδρῶν τε θεῶν τε.

Od. Σ. 129.

VERGIL

Remember that these reproaches have to be made more
sparingly by men.

What can the masters do, when thieves are so bold.

Cruel love, to what extremities doth thou drive the
hearts of men !

Why delay ?   Woman is always a changing and inconstant thing.

VERGIL,

Parcius ista viris tamen objicienda memento.

Virg. Ecl. 3. 7.

Quid domini faciant, audent,cum talia fures.

Id. 3, 16,

Improbe amor,quid non mortalia pectora cogis.

AE. 4.412.

Eia age, rumpe moras ; varium et mutabile semper Femina....

AE. 4. 564.

HORACE

The snows have fled ; already the grass is returning to the fields and a mane of leaves to the trees.

A dreadful storm has narrowed the horizon ; the snows and the rains are falling from the skies.

O daughter even more beautiful than your beautiful mother.

But through resignation even that grows lighter which Heaven forbids us to remedy (death).

Pale Death knocks equally at the door of the poor man's cabin and at the palaces of the rulers.

Enjoy to-day and put as little trust as possible in the morrow.

O brave companions, who with me have suffered so much more, drown your cares in wine. . To-morrow we shall sail the immense sea again.

HORATIUS (1)

Diffugere nives, redeunt gramina campis
Arboribusque comæ.   [*Lib. IV, Ode* 7.]

Horrida tempestas cœlum contraxit, et imbres
Nivesque deducunt Jovem.   [*Epod. XI, v.* 407.]

O, matre pulchrâ, filia pulchrior.   [*Lib. I, Ode* 16.]

.....Sed levius fit patientia,
Quicquid corripere est nefas.   *Lib. I. Ode* 24.

Pallida mors æquo pulsat pede pauperum tabernas
Regumque turreis.....   *Lib. I. Ode* 4.

...Carpe diem, quam minimum credula postero.
                                Lib. I. Ode 11.

O fortes pejoraque passi
Mecum sæpe viri, nunc vino pellite curas :
Cras ingens iterabimus æquor.   *Lib. I. Ode* 7. (2)

(1) Very early writing.
(2) Later writing as well as the quotations from Horace that follow.

The man who tears to pieces a friend behind his back,. or does not stand for him when he is accused ; the man who seeks to make people laugh to acquire the name of a good story-teller; he who can imagine what he has not seen and cannot keep secrets entrusted to him, such a man has a dark soul.   Keep away from him, O Roman.

O country when shall I see you again ?   When shall I be permitted to read the books of the ancient writers or,. giving to sleep drowsy hours, to enjoy the sweet oblivion of a restless existence.

All earthly beings have received only perishable lives and neither the great nor the poor can escape death.. And so, dear friend, enjoy all the good things in life, and while you live remember that life is short.

Now what man is free ?   The wise man who rules. himself, afraid neither of poverty, death or prison ; who has enough strength to check his passions and scorn honors ; who is self sufficient ; who offers to external. accident no hold and whom chance cannot catch unaware..

.....Add to that the fact that you cannot stay a single hour by yourself ; that you do not know how to enjoy honestly your leisure ; that you try to escape from yourself as a fugitive slave and seek relief from your restlessness in wine or sleep.   All in vain ! the somber companion. pursues and urges on the fugitive !

...Absentem qui rodit amicum,
Qui non defendit, alio culpante ; solutos
Qui captat risus hominum, famanque dicacis ;
Fingere qui non visa potest, commissa tacere
Qui nequit, hic niger est : hunc tu Romane cáveto (1)..

> *Satyr. Lib.* i. *Sat* : 4, *l.* 81.

O rus quando te aspiciam ? Quandoque licebit
Nunc veterum libris, nunc somno et inertibus horis
Ducere sollicitæ jucunda oblivia vitæ ?

> *Lib.* 2. *Sat.* 6, *v.* 60.

.....terrestria quando
Mortales animas vivunt sortita, neque ulla est
Aut magno aut parvo lethi fuga : quo, bone, circa,
Dum licet, in rebus jucundis vive beatus :
Vive memor, quam sis ævi brevis.

> *Id. v.* 93.

Quisnam igitur liber ?   Sapiens ; sibi qui imperiosus
Quem neque pauperies,neque mors,neque vincula terrent ;
Responsare cupidinibus, contemnere honores
Fortis ; et in seipso totus, teres atque rotundus,
Externi ne quid valeat per læve morari ;
In quem manca ruit semper fortuna.

> *Sat* : 7, *v.* 83. *Lib.* 2.

.....Adde   quod   idem
Non horam tecum esse potes, non otia recte
Ponere ; teque ipsum vitas fugitivus et erro ;
Jam vino quærens, jam somno fallere curam :
Frustra : nam comes atra premit, sequiturque fugacem..

> *Id. v.* 111.

(1) Quoted again in a letter to James Madison. Aug. 28, 1789. *M. E.*.
VII, 444.

TERENTIUS

When the mind is in doubt little suffices to carry it hither and thither.

It is easy when we are in good health to give good advice to the sick.

TERENTIUS (1)

Dum in dubio est animus, paulo momento huc vel illuc impellitur.

> *Ter. And.*[*ria. I, v.* 31.]

Facile omnes, cum valemus, recta consilia ægrotis damus.

> *Id.* [*II,* 1, 9.]

(1) Early writing.

OVID : EPISTLES (HEROIDS)

One must easily bear whatever one deserves, but undeserved punishment brings with it grief.

What a pity love cannot be cured with simples.

Whatever will happen will be better than what is now.

But I am unskillful at concealment.   Who indeed could conceal a fire that betrays itself by its light.

OVID : EPIST. (1)

Leniter, ex merito quicquid patiare, ferendum est :
Quæ venit indignæ pæna, dolenda venit.

Œnon. Par. v. 7.

Me miseram, quod Amor mon est medicabilis herbis !

Id. 123

Quidquid erit, melius quam nunc erit.

Sappho. Phaon.

Sed male dissimulo : quis enim celaverit ignem
Lumine qui semper proditur ipse suo.

Par. Helen.

(1) Very early writing.

But should this Arm prepare to wreak our hate
On thy lov'd Realms, whose Guilt demands their fate
Presume not thou the lifted Bolt to stay,
Remember TROY, and give the Vengeance way.

Iliad : 4. *l*: 61.

'Tis not in me the Vengeance to remove :
The Crime's sufficient that they share my Love.

Id. : *l* : 79.

Say, is it thus those Honours you requite ?
The first in Banquets, but the last in Fight.

Id : *l* : 400.

Who dares think one Thing, and another tell,
My heart detests him as the Gates of Hell.

Il : 9. *l* : 412.

The Wife whom Choice and passion both approve,
Sure every wise and worthy Man will love.
Nor did my fair one less Distinction claim ;
Slave as she was my Soul ador'd the Dame.

Id : *l* : 450.

(1) Very early writing.

There deaf for ever to the Martial Strife,
Enjoy the dear prerogative of Life.
Life is not to be bought with heaps of Gold.
Not all Apollo's Pythian Treasures hold,
Or Troy once held, in peace and pride of sway.
Can bribe the poor possession of a Day !

Id : l : 523.

Yet hear one Word, and lodge it in thy Heart ;
No more molest me on Atrides' part :
It is for him these Tears are taught to flow,
For him these sorrows ? for my mortal Foe ?
A Gen'rous Freindship no cold medium knows,
Burns with one Love, with one Resentment glows,
One should our Int'rests, and our passions be ;
My Friend must hate the Man that injures me.

Id : l : 721.

..................but at the Tyrant's Name
My Rage rekindles, and my soul's on flame :
'Tis just Resentment, and becomes the brave ;
Disgrac'd, dishonour'd like the vilest slave.

Id : l : 759.

Then none (said Nestor) shall his Rule withstand
For great Examples justify Command.

Il : 10. *l :* 148

Death is the worst ; a Fate which all must try ;
And, for our Country, 'tis a Bliss to die.
The gallant Man tho' slain in Fight he be,
Yet leaves his Nation safe, his Children free ;
Entails a Debt on all the gratefull State ;
His own brave Friends shall glory in his Fate :
His Wife live Honour'd, all his Race succeed ;
And late Posterity enjoy the Deed.

Il : 15. *l:* 582.

On Valour's Side, the Odds of Combate lie,
The brave live glorious, or lamented die;
The Wretch that trembles in the Field of Fame,
Meets Death, & worse than Death, eternal shame.

Id : l : 670.

For ah ! what is there, of inferiour Birth,
That breathes or creeps upon the Dust of Earth ;
What wretched Creature of what wretched Kind,
Than Man more weak, calamitous, and blind ?
A miserable Race !

Il : 17. *l:* 508.

What art thou, speak, that on Designs unknown
While others sleep, thus range the Camp alone ?
Seek'st thou some Friend or nightly Centinel ?
Stand off, approach not, but thy purpose tell.

Il : 10. *l.* 90.

These shall I slight ?　And guide my wav'ring Mind
By wan'dring Birds that flit with ev'ry Wind ?
Ye Vagrants of the Sky !　your Wings extend
Or where the Suns arise, or where descend ;
To Right, to Left, unheeded take your Way
While I the Dictates of high Heav'n obey.
Without a Sign his Sword the brave Man draws
And asks no Omen but his Country's Cause.

Il : 12. *l :* 277.

Lost herds and treasures, we by arms regain,
And steeds unrivall'd on the dusty plain :·
But from our lips the vital spirit fled,
Returns no more to wake the silent dead.

Il : 9. *v.* 528.

To labour is the lot of man below ;
And when Jove, gave us life, he gave us woe.

Il : 10 *v.* 78.

POPE'S HOMER

Could all our care elude the gloomy grave,
Which claims no less the fearful than the brave,
For lust of fame, I should not vainly dare
In fighting fields, nor urge thy soul to war.
But since, alas ! ignoble age must come,
Disease, and death's inexorable doom ;
The life which others pay let us bestow,
And give to fame what we to nature owe ;

Il : 12. v. 307.

................Let reason mitigate our care :
To mourn, avails not : man is born to bear.
Such is, alas ! the gods severe decree ;
They, only they, are blest, and only free.
Two urns by Jove's high throne have ever stood,
The source of evil one, the one of good ;
From thence the cup of mortal man he fills.
Blessings to these, to those distributes ills ;
To most, he mingles both : the wretch decreed
To taste the bad, unmix'd, is curst indeed ;
Pursu'd by wrongs, by meagre famine driv'n.
He wanders, outcast both of earth and heav'n.
The happiest taste not happiness sincere,
But find the cordial draught is dash'd with care.

B. 24. v. 659.

POPE'S ESSAY ON MAN (1)

If to be perfect in a certain Sphere
What matters soon, or late, or here, or there,
The blest to Day is as completely so,
As who began a Thousand Years ago.

Ep : 1. *v* : 73.

For morè Perfection than this State can bear
In vain we sigh ; Heaven made us as we are.
As Wisely sure a modest Ape might aim
To be like Man.

Ep : 2. *v*. 19.

Fools who from hence into the Notion fall
That Vice or Virtue there is none at all.
If white, & black, blend, soften & Unite
A thousand Ways ; is there no black or White ?
Ask your own Heart, ?& Nothing is so plain ;
'Tis to mistake them, costs the Time & Pain.

Ep. : 2. *v*. 211.

What we resolve, we can : but here's the Fault,
We ne'er resolve to do the Thing we ought.
Heaven forming each on other to depend,
A Master, or a Servant, or a Friend,
Bids each on other for assistance call,
Till one Man's Weakness grows ye Strength of all.

Ep : 2. *v* : 249.

(1) Early writing, apparently of the same date as the preceding quotations.

Whate'r the Passion, Knowledge, Fame or Pelf
Not one will change his Neighbour for himself.
The learn'd is happy Nature to explore,
The Fool is happy that he knows no more,
The Rich is happy in the plenty Given,
The Poor contents him with the Care of Heavn
See the blind Beggar dance, the Cripple sing,
The Sot a Hero, Lunatic a King ;
The starving Chymist in his golden Views
Supremely blest, the Poet in his Muse,
See some strange Comfort ev'ry state attend,
And pride bestow'd on all, a common Friend
See some fit passion ev'ry Age supply,
Hope travels thro', nor quits us when we die.
Behold the Child, by Nature's kindly Law,
Pleas'd with a Rattle, tickl'd with a Straw.
Some livelier Plaything gives his Youth Delight
A little louder, but as empty quite :
Scarfs, Garters, Gold, amuse his riper Stage,
And Beads & Prayer-books are the Toys of Age :
Pleas'd with this Bauble still, as that before ;
Till tir'd he sleeps, & Life's poor Play is o'er.

Ep : 2. *v* : 261.

Say not, " Heav'n's here profuse, there poorly saves,
And for one Monarch makes a Thousand Slaves. "
You'll find, when Causes & their Ends are known,
T'was for the Thousand Heav'n made has that one.

Ep : 4. *v* : 53.

Fortune her Gifts may variously dispose,
And these be happy call'd, unhappy those ;
But Heaven's just Balance equal will appear
While those are plac'd in Hope, & these in Fear :
Not present Good or Ill, the Joy or Curse,
But future Views of better, or of worse.

Ep : 4. *v* : 67.

Honour & shame from no Condition rise ;
Act well your Part, there all the Honour lies
Fortune in Men has some small Difference made
One flaunts in Rags, one flutters in Brocade.
The Cobler apron'd, & the Parson gown'd,
The Friar hooded, & the Monarch crown'd,
" What differ more, you say, than Crown & Cowl. "
I'll tell you Friend. — A wise Man & a Fool.

Ep : 4. *v* : 193.

Go ; if your antient, but ignoble Blood
Has crept thro' Scoundrels ever since the Flood ;
Go ! & pretend your Family is Young ;
Nor own, your Fathers have been Fools so long :
What can ennoble Sots, or Slaves, or Cowards ?
Alas ! not all the Blood of all the Howards.

Ep : 4. *v* : 211.

Not one looks backward, onward still he goes ;
Yet ne'er looks forward further than his Nose.

Ep : 4. *v*. 223.

[SAMUEL BUTLER] (1)

Tho' we with blacks & blues are suggil'd,
Or, as the vulgar say, are cudgel'd :
He that is valiant dares fight
Tho' drubb'd, can lose no honor by't.

Hudibr. 3. 1039

If he that is in battle slain
Be in the bed of honor lain ;
He that is beaten, may be said
To lie in honour's truckle bed.

id. 3. 1047.

For Wedlock, without love, some say,
Is but a lock without a key.

id. part. 2. *Canto* 1.321.

Those that fly may fight again,
Which he can never do that's slain.

ib. 243.

(1) Later writing than the quotations from Pope.

MILTON'S PARADISE LOST. (1)

.... Round he threw his baleful Eyes
That witness'd huge Affliction & Dismay.

Lib : I. l. 56.

............What tho the Field be lost ?
All is not lost ; the unconquerable Will,
And Study of Revenge, immortal Hate
And Courage never to submit or yield :
And what is else not to be overcome ?
That Glory never shall his Wrath or Might
Extort from me. To bow & Sue for Grace
With suppliant knee, & deifie his Power
Who from the Terrour of this Arm : so late
Doubted his Empire, that were low indeed
That were an Ignominy, & shame beneath
This Downfall.

Id : l. 105.

................But of this be sure
To do ought Good never will be our Task
But ever to do Ill our sole Delight,
As being contrary to his high Will
Whom we resist...............

Id : l. 158.

(1) Early writing.

Here we may reign secure, & in my Choice
To reign is worth Ambition tho' in Hell,
Better to reign in Hell, than serve in Heaven.

Lib : 1. *l.* 261.

...............But he his wonted pride
Soon recollecting, with high words that bore
Semblance of Worth, not Substance, gently rais'd
Their fainting Courage, & dispell'd their Fears.

Id : *l.* 527.

...............Our better part remains
To work in close Design, by Fraud or Guile,
What Force effected not : that he no less
At length from us may find, who overcomes
By Force, hath overcome but half his Foe.

Lib : *I* : *v.* 645.

...............though in this vast Recess,
Free, & to none accountable, preferring
Hard Liberty before the easy Yoke
Of servile Pomp.

Lib : 2. *v.* 254

Nor gentle purpose, nor endearing smiles
Wanted, nor youthful dalliance as beseems
Fair couple, linkt in happy nuptial league.
Alone as they................

Milton. Par. L. 4. 337 (1)

(1) Different and probably later writing. This quotation is separated
from the others by a blank page.

...............if I must contend, said he
Best with the best ; the sender not the sent,
Or all at once ; more glory will be won,
Or less be lost.

Milt. Par. L. 4.851.

...............well we may afford
Our givers their own gifts, & large bestow
From large bestow'd.

id. 5.316.

...............but in those hearts
Love unlibidinous reign'd, nor jealousy
Was understood, the injur'd lover's hell.

id. 5. 448.

...............One who brings
A mind not to be chang'd by place or time
The mind is it's own place, & in itself
Can make a Heav'n of Hell, a Hell of Heav'n.

Milt. Par. L. B. I. l : 252.

Reign thou in Hell thy Kingdom, let me serve
In Heav'n God ever blest, & his divine
Behests obey, worthiest to be obey'd,
Yet Chains in Hell, not Realms expect.

B : 6. *l* : 183.

Nameless in dark Oblivion let them dwell.

Id. l : 380.

Nor long shall be our Labour, yet e'er Dawn
Effect shall end our Wish.   Meanwhile revive ;
Abandon Fear ; to Strength & Counsel join'd
Think Nothing hard, much less to be dispair'd.

Id. l : 492.

But apt the Mind or Fancy is to rove
Uncheckt, & of her roving is no End ;
Till warn'd, or by Experience taught, she learn
That not to know at large of Things remote
From Use, obscure & subtle, but to know
That which before us lies in daily Life,
Is the prime Wisdom, what is more, is fume
Or Emptiness, or fond Impertinence,
And renders us in Things that most concern
Unpractis'd, unprepar'd, & still to seek.
Therefore from this high Pitch let us descend
A lower Flight, & speak of Things at Hand
Useful. . . . .

$B : 8. \ l : 188.$

Among Unequals what Society
Can sort, what Harmony or true Delight ?
Which must be mutual, in Proportion due
Giv'n & receiv'd ; but in Disparity.
The one intense, the other still remiss
Cannot well suit with either, but soon prove
Tedious alike :. . . . .

$Id : l : 383.$

. . . . .here Passion first I felt,
Commotion strange, in all Enjoyments else
Superior & unmov'd, here only weak
Against the Charm of Beautie's powerful Glance
Or Nature fail'd in me, & left some Part
Not proof enough such Object to sustain,
Or from my Side subducting, took perhaps
More than enough ; at least on her bestow'd
Too much of Ornament, in outward Shew
Elaborate :. . . . .

$Id : l : 530.$

For what admir'st thou, what transports Thee so
An Outside ?   fair no Doubt, & worthy well
Thy cherishing, thy honouring, & thy Love,
Not thy Subjection : weigh with her thyself ;
Then value : Oft-times nothing profits more
Than Self-esteem, grounded on just & right
Well manag'd ; of that skill the more thou know'st
The more she will acknowledge thee her Head,
And to Realities yield all her shows ;
Made so adorn for thy Delight the more,
So awful, that with Honour thou may'st love
Thy Mate, who sees when thou art seen least wise.

Id : *l* : 567.

For he who tempts, though in vain, at least asperses
The tempted with Dishonour foul, suppos'd
Not incorruptible of Faith, not Proof
Against temptation.

[*B*. 9. *l*. 296].

..............Thus it shall befal
Him who to Worth in Women overtrusting
Lets her Will rule ; restraint she will not brook,
And left to herself, if Evil thence ensue,
The first his weak Indulgence will accuse.

Id : *l* : 1182.

But past who can recall, or done undo ?
Not God omnipotent, nor Fate.

Id : *l* : 926.

Be it so ! for I submit ; His Doom is fair,
That Dust I am, & shall to Dust return.
O welcome Hour whenever !   Why delays
His Hand to execute, what His Decree
Fix'd on this Day ?   Why do I over-live ?
Why am I mock'd with Death, & lengthen'd out

To deathless Pain ? How gladly would I meet
Mortality my Sentence, & be Earth
Insensible ! How glad would lay me down,
As in my Mother's Lap ! There I should rest
And sleep secure : His dreadful Voice no more
Would thunder in my Fears : . . . .

B : 10. *l* : 769.

. . . . .imagin'd wise,
Constant, mature, proof against all Assaults :
And understood not all was but a shew,
Rather than solid Virtue ; all but a Rib,
Crooked by Nature, bent (as now appears)
More to the Part sinister from me drawn ;
Well if thrown out, as supernumerary
To my just Number found ! — O ! why did God,
Creator wise ! that Peopl'd highest Heav'n
With spirits masculine, create at last
This Novelty on Earth, this fair Defect
Of Nature ?   And not fill the world at once
With Men, as Angels, without feminine ?
Or find some other Way to generate
Mankind ?   This Mischeif had not then befall'n
And more that shall befal : innumerable
Disturbances on Earth through female Snares,
And straight Conjunction with this Sex ! . . . . . .

[*B*. 10. *l* : 881].

. . . . .let us make short,
Let us seek DEATH : — or, he not found, supply
With our own Hands his Office on ourselves.
Why stand we longer shivering under Fears,
That shew no End but Death ; & have the Pow'r
Of many Ways to die, the shortest chusing,
Destruction with Destruction to Destroy ?

Id : *l* : 1000.

But have I now seen Death ? is this the Way
I must return to native Dust ?   O sight
Of Terror, foul, & ugly to behold,
Horrid to think, how horrible to feel.

B. .11 l. 462.

At length a reverend Sire among them came,
And of their Doings great Dislike declar'd,
And testify'd against their Ways : he oft
Frequented their Assemblies, whereso met,
Triumphs, or Festivals ; & to them preach'd
Conversion & Repentance ;

Id. : l. 719.

...Let no Man seek
Henceforth to be foretold, what shall befall
Him or his Children : Evil he may be sure :
Which neither his foreknowing can prevent,
And he the future Evil shall no less
In Apprehension, than in Substance, feel ;

Id : l : 770.

...since with Sorrow, & Heart's Distress
Wearied I fell asleep : but now, lead on !
In me is no Delay ; with thee to go,
Is to stay here ; wihtout thee here to stay,
Is to go hence unwilling : thou to me
Art all Things under Heav'n ; all places thou.

B : 12. *l.* 613.

[YOUNG]

Youth is not rich in time, it may be poor ;
Part with it as with money, sparing ; pay
No moment but in purchase of it's worth ;
And what it's worth, ask death-beds ; they can tell.
Part with it as with life, reluctant ; big
With holy hope of nobler time to come.

Young's N. T. night. 2.

Time's use was doom'd a pleasure : waste, a pain
That man might feel his error if unseen :
And, feeling, fly to labor for his cure ;
Not, blund'ring, split on idleness for ease.
Life's cares are comforts ; such by heav'n design'd ;
He that has none must make them or be wretched.
Cares are emploiments ; and without employ
The soul is on a rack ; the rack of rest,
To souls most adverse ; action all their joy.   *Id. Ib.*

Speech ventilates our intellectual fire ;
Speech burnishes our mental magazine ;
Brightens for ornament ; and whets for use.
What numbers'sheath'd in erudition, lie,
Plung'd to the hilts in venerable tomes,
And rusted in ; who might have borne an edge,
And play'd a sprightly beam, if born' to speech ;
If born blest heirs of half their mother's tongue !
" 'Tis thought's exchange, which, like th'alternate push
Of waves conflicting, breaks the learned scum,
And defecates the student's standing pool.   *Id. Ib.*

Nature, in zeal for human amity,
Denies, or damps, and undivided joy.
Joy is an import ; joy is an exchange ;
Joy flies monopolists : it calls for two ;

Id. Ib.

O ! lost to virtue, lost to manly thought,
Lost to the noble sallies of the soul !!
Who think it solitude to be alone.
Communion sweet ! communion large and high !
Our reason, guardian angel, and our god !
Then nearest these, when others most remote ;
And all, ere long, shall be remote but these.

Id. Night. 3.

Woes cluster ; rare are solitary woes ;
They love a train, they tread each other's heel ;

Id. Ib.

Ye that e'er lost an angel ! pity me.

Id. Ib.

For what live ever here ? with lab'ring step
To tread our former footsteps ?   Pace the round
Eternal ?   to climb life's worn, heavy wheel,
Which draws up nothing new ? to beat, and beat
The beaten track ? to bid each wretched day
The former mock ? to surfeit on the same,
And yawn our joys ? or thank a misery
For change, tho' sad ? To see what we have seen ?
Hear, till unhear'd the same old slabber'd tale ?
To taste the tasted, and at each return
Less tasteful ? o'er our palates to decant
Another vintage ? strain a flatter year
Thro' loaded vessels, and a laxer tone ?

Id. Ib.

A truth it is, few doubt, but fewer trust,
" He sins against this life, who slights the next. "

Id. Ib.

A languid, leaden, iteration reigns
And ever must, o'er those, whose joys are joys
Of sight, smell, taste : the cuckow seasons sings
The same dull note to such as nothing prize,
But what those seasons, from the teeming earth,
To doating sense indulge, but nobler minds,
Which relish fruits unripen'd by the sun,
Make their days various ; various as the dyes
On the dove's neck, which wanton in his rays.

Id. Ib.

Why start at death ? where is he ? death arriv'd
Is past ; not come, or gone, he's never here.
Ere hope, sensation fails ; black-boding man
Receives, not suffers, death's tremendous blow
The knell, the shroud, the mattock, and the grave ;
The deep damp vault, the darkness, and the worm ;
These are the bugbears of a winter's eve.
The terrors of the living, not the dead.
Imagination's foot, and error's wretch,
Man makes a death which nature never made ;
Then on the point of his own fancy falls ;
And feels a thousand death's in fearing one.

Id. Night. 4.

Death ! great Proprietor of all ! tis thine
To tread out Empire, & to quench the Stars.
The Sun himself by thy Permission shines ;
And, one Day, thou shalt pluck him from his sphere
Amid such mighty plunder, why exhaust
They partial Quiver on a Mark so mean ?
Why thy peculiar Rancour wreck'd on me ?
Insatiate Archer could not one suffice ?
Thy Shaft flew thrice, & thrice my Peace was slain
And thrice, e'er thrice yon Moon fill'd her Horn.

L[ife] D[eath] & Immortality

Know'st thou, Lorenzo ! what a Freind contains
As Bees mixt Nectar draw from fragrant Flow'rs
To Men from Friendship, Wisdom & Delight ;
Twins ty'd by Nature ; if they part they die.
Hast thou no Freind to set thy Mind abroach
Good Sense will stagnate, Thoughts shut up, want Air
And spoil like Bales unopen'd to the Sun.

L : D : Friendship.

A Soul immortal spending all her Fires ;
Wasting her Strength in strenuous Idleness,
Thrown into Tumult, raptur'd, or alarm'd,
As ought this Scene can threaten, or indulge,
Resembles Ocean into Tempest wrought,
To waft a Feather, or to drown a Fly.

L : D : Immort.

⟨1⟩ Earlier writing.

What Numbers once in Fortune's Lap high-fed,
Sollicit the cold Hand of Charity !
To shock us more, sollicit it in vain !

Id :

Tir'd nature's sweet restorer, balmy sleep !
He, like the world, his ready visit pays
Where fortune smiles ; the wretched he forsakes ;
Swift on his downy pinion flies from woe,
And lights on lids unsullied with a tear.

Id. Ib.

The cobwed'b cottage, with it's ragged wall
Of mould'ring mud, is royalty to me !
The spider's most attenuated thread
Is cord, is cable to man's tender tie
On earthly bliss ; it breaks at every breeze.

Id. Ib.

Misfortune, like a creditor severe,
But rises in demand for her delay ;
She makes a scourge of past prosperity,
To sling thee more, and double thy distress.

Id. Ib.

By nature's law, what may be, may be now ;
There's no prerogative in human hours.
In human hearts what bolder thought can rise,
Than man's presumption on tomorrow's dawn ?
Where is tomorrow ? in another world.
For numbers this is certain ; the reverse
Is sure to none ; and yet on this perhaps,
This peradventure, infamous for lies,
As on a rock of adamant we build
Our mountain hopes ; spin out eternal schemes,
As we the fatal sisters could outspin,
And, big with life's futurities, expire.

Id. Ib (1).

(1) Quoted in *Thoughts on English Prosody*, *M. E.* XVIII, 437.

Be wise today ; tis madness to defer ;
Next day the fatal precedent will plead ;
Thus on till wisdom is pushd' out of life.
Procrastination is the thief of time ;
Year after year it steals, till all are fled,
And to the mercies of a moment leaves
The vast concerns of an eternal scene.
If not so frequent, would not this be strange ?
That, tis so frequent, this is stranger still.
Of man's miraculous mistakes, this bears
The palm 'that all men are about to live',
For ever on the brink of being born.

Id. Ib.

All promise is poor dilatory man,
And that thro' every stage : when young, indeed,
In full content we, sometimes, nobly rest,
Unanxious for ourselves ; and only wish,
As duteous sons, our fathers were more wise.
At thirty man suspects himself a fool ;
Knows it at forty, and reforms his plan ;
At fifty chides his infamous delay,
Pushes his prudent purpose to resolve ;
In all the magnanimity of thought
Resolves ; and re-resolves ; then dies the same.
And why ? because he thinks himself immortal.
All men think all men mortal, but themselves ;
Themselves, when some alarming stroke of fate
Strikes thro' their wounded, heart the sudden dread ;
But their hearts wounded, like the wounded air,
Soon close ; where past the shaft no trace is found.
As from the wing no scar the sky retains ;
The parted wave no furrow from the keel ;
So dies in human hearts the thought of death.
Ev'n with the tender tear which nature sheds
O'er those we love, we drop it in their grave.

Young's N. T. night. 1.

SHAKESPEAR (1)

Cowards die many Times before their Deaths ;
The valiant never taste of Death but once.
Of all the wonders that I yet have heard,
It seems to me most strange that Men should fear
Seeing that Death, a necessary End,
Will come when it will come.

Julius Cæsar. Act. 2. Scene 4 :

Must I give Way & Room to your rash Choler ?
Shall I be frighted when a Madman stares ?

Fret 'till your proud Heart break :
Go shew your Slaves how choleric you are,
And make your Bond-men tremble.   Must I budge ?
Must I observe you ?   Must I stand & crouch
Under your testy Humour ?   By the Gods,
You shall digest the Venom of your Spleen,
Tho' it do split you : For from this Day forth,
I'll use you for my Mirth, yea, for my Laughter,
When you are waspish.

Id. Act. 4. *S* : 3.

Do not presume too much upon my Love ;
I may do that I shall be sorry for.

Id.

(1) Very early writing.

I cannot tell, what you & other Men
Think of this Life ; but for my single self,
I had as lief not be, as live to be
In awe of such a Thing as I myself.
I was born free as Cæsar, so were you ;
We both have fed as well ; & we can both
Endure the Winter's cold as well as he.

    . . . . . . This Man
Is now become a God, & Cassius is
A wretched Creature, & must bend his Body,
If Cæsar carelesly but nod on him.

Id : Act. 1. Sc : 3.

    ...Hold my Hand :
Be factious for Redress of all these Griefs,
And I will this Foot of mine as far,
As who goes farthest.

Id : Sc : 7

That we shall die, we know ; tis but the time,
And drawing Days out, that Men stand upon
And, he that cuts off twenty Years of Life,
Cutts of so many Years of fearing Death.
Grant that & then is Death a Benefit.

Id : Act. 3. Sc. 2.

If we are mark'd to die, we are enow
To do our Country Loss ; & if to live,
The fewer Men, the greater Share of Honour.
God's Will ! I pray thee wish not one Man more.

Shakespear. [Henry IV, Part, 1 sc. 1].

But if it be a Sin to covet Honour,
I am the most offending Soul alive.

Id : [Henry IV, Part 1, Act. 3, sc. 1].

. . . . . Honour pricks me on. But how if
Honour prick me off, when I come on ? how then ?
Can Honour set a Leg ?   No : or an Arm ?   No :
Or take away the Greif of a wound ? No : Honour
hath no Skill in Surgery then ?   No : What is
Honour ?   A word : What is that Word Honour ?
Air ; a trim Reckoning. Who hath it ?   He
that died a Wednesday.   Doth he feel it ? No :
Doth he hear it ?   No :   Is it insensible then ?
Yea, to the Dead : But will it not live with the
Living ?   No.   Why ? Detraction will not suf-[fer it.
Therefore I'll none of it ; Honour is a
meer scutcheon, and so ends my catechism.

> *Henry* 4th. *Part* 1 st. *Act* : 5. *Sc.* : 2.

...Extremity was the Trier of spirits,
That common Chances common Men could bear ;
That when the Sea was calm, all Boats alike,
Shew'd Mastership in floating ; Fortune's Blows
When most struck Home, being greatly warded, crave[s
A noble Cunning.

> *Coriolanus. Act.* 4. *Sc* : 1.

I wish the Gods had nothing else to do
But to confirm my Curses.

> *Id* : *Sc.* 2.

He was not taken well, he had not din'd.
The Veins unfill'd, Our Blood is cold, & then,
We pout upon the morning, are unapt,
To give, or to forgive ; but when we've stuff'd
These Pipes, & these Conveyances of Blood
With Wine & Feeding, we have supler Souls
Than in our Priest-like Fasts.

> *Id* : *Act* : 5. *Sc* : 1.

. . . . . Shall remain ?
Hear you this Triton of the Minnows ? mark you
His absolute Shall ? . . . . .
. . . . . Shall ?
O ! good, but most unwise Patricians, why,
You grave but reckless Senators, have you thus
Given Hydra here to chuse an Officer,
That with his peremptory Shall, being but
The Horn & Noise o'th' Monsters, wants not Spirit
To say he'll turn your Current in a Ditch,
And make your Channel his ? if they have power
Let them have Cushions by you : if none, awake
Your dang'rous Levity : if you are learned,
Be not as common Fools ; if you are not,
Then vail your Ignorance. . . . .
. . . . . They chuse their Magistrate,
And such a one as he, who puts his Shall,
His popular Shall, against a graver Bench
Than ever frown'd in Greece.

Id : Act : 3. Sc. 1.

What stronger Breast-plate than a Heart untainted ?
Thrice is he arm'd that has his Quarrel just ;
And he but naked though lock'd up in Steel,
Whose Conscience with Injustice is corrupted.

Hen : VI th.

. . . . . In struggling with Misfortunes
Lies the true proof of Virtue. On smooth Seas
How many Bawble Boats dare set their sails,
And make an equal way with firmer Vessels :
But let the Tempest once enrage the Sea,
And then behold the string ribb'd Argosie
Bounding between the Ocean & the Air,
Like Perseus mounted on his Pegasus ;
Then where are those weak Rivals of the Main ?

Or to avoid the Tempest fled to port,
Or made a prey to Neptune.   Even thus
Do empty shew & true-priz'd Worth divide
In storms of Fortune.....

Troilus & Cressida.

Even love itself is bitterness of soul,
A pleasing anguish pining at the heart.

Spring v. 338.

. . . . . Ah then, ye fair !
Be greatly cautious of your sliding hearts ;
Dare not the infectious sigh ; the pleading eye,
In meek submission drest, deject, and low,
But full of tempting guile. Let not the tongue,
Prompt to deceive, with adulation smooth,
Gain on your purpos'd will. Nor in the bower,
Where woodbines flaunt, and roses shed a couch
While evening draws her crimson curtains round,
Trust your soft minutes with betraying man.
And let th'aspiring youth beware of love,
Of the smooth glance beware ; for 'tis too late,
When on his heart the torrent softness pours.
Then wisdom prostrate lies ; and fading fame.
Dissolves in air away : while the fond soul
Is wrapt in dreams of ecstacy, and bliss ;
Still paints th'illusive form ; the kindling grace ;
Th'inticing smile ; the modest-seeming eye,
Beneath whose beauteous beams, belying heaven,
Lurk searchless cunning, cruelty and death.
And still, false-warbling in his cheated ear,
Her syren voice, enchanting draws him on,
To guileful shores, and meads of fatal joy.

Id : *v.* 887..

(1) Early writing.

But absent, what fantastick pangs arrous'd,
Rage in each thought, by restless musing fed,
Chill the warm cheek, and blast the bloom of life !
Neglected fortune flies ; and sliding swift,
Prone into ruin, fall his scorn'd affairs.
'Tis nought but gloom around.   The darken'd sun
Loses his light.   The rosy bosom'd Spring
To weeping fancy pines ; and yon bright arch
Of heav'n, low bends into a dusty vault.
All nature fades extinct ; and she alone
Heard, felt, and seen, possesses every thought,
Fills every sense, and pants in every vein.
Books are but formal dulness, tedious friends,
And sad amid the social band he sits,
Lonely, and inattentive.   From the tongue
Th'unfinish'd period falls : while, born away
On swelling thought, his wafted spirit flies
To the vain bosom of his distant fair ;
And leaves the semblance of a lover, fix'd
In melancholy site, with head declin'd.
And love-dejected eyes.   Sudden he starts,
Shook from his tender trance, and restless runs
To glimmering shades, and sympathetic glooms,
Where the dun umbrage o'er the falling stream
Romantic hangs ; there thro' the pensive dusk
Strays, in heart-thrilling meditation lost,
Indulging all to love : or on the bank
Thrown, amid drooping lillies, swells the breeze
With sighs unceasing, and the brook with tears.
Thus in soft anguish he consumes the day,
Nor quits his deep retirement, till the moon
Peeps thro' the chambers of the fleecy east,
Enlighten'd by degrees, and in her train
Leads on the gentle hours ; then forth he walks,
Beneath the trembling languish of her beams,
With soften'd soul, and wooes the bird of eve
To mingle woes with his : or while the world,
And all the sons of care, lie hush'd in sleep,

Associates with the midnight shadows drear ;
And sighing to the lonely taper, pours
His idly-tortur'd heart into the page,
Meant for the moving messenger of love ;
Where rapture burns on rapture, every line
With rising frenzy fir'd. But if on bed
Delirious flung, sleep from his pillow flies.
All night he tosses, nor the balmy power
In any posture finds ; till the grey morn
Lifts her pale lustre on the paler wretch,
Exanimate by love : and then perhaps
Exhausted nature sinks a while to rest,
Still interrupted by distracted dreams,
That o'er the sick imagination rise,
And in black colors paint the mimic scene.
Oft with th'enchantress of his soul he talks ;
Sometimes in crowds distress'd ; or if retir'd
To secret-winding, flower-enwoven bowers,
Far from the dull impertinence of man,
Just as he, credulous, his thousand cares
Begins to lose in blind oblivious love,
Snatch'd from her yeilding hand, he knows not how
Through forests huge, and long untravel'd heath
With desolation brown, he wanders waste,
In night and tempest wrapt ; or shrinks aghast
Back, from the bending precipice ; or wades
The turbid stream below, and strives to reach
The farther shore ; where succorless, and sad,
Wild as a Bacchanal she spreads her arms,
But strives in vain, born by th'outrageous flood
To distance down, he rides the ridgy wave,
Orwhelm'd beneath the boiling eddy sinks.
Then a weak, wailing, lamentable cry
Is heard, and all in tears he wakes, again
To tread the circle revolving woe.
These are the charming agonies of love,
Whose misery delights.

Id : *v.* : 918.

ENGLISH DRAMAS

. . . . . It wounds indeed
To bear affronts, too great to be forgiven,
And not have power to punish.

Dryd[en] Spa[nish]. Fryar.

Fortune takes care that Fools should still be seen ;
She places them aloft, o'th'topmost Spoke
Of all her Wheel. Fools are the daily Work
Of Nature, her Vocation. If she form
A Man, she loses by it ; 'tis too expensive ;
'Twould make ten Fools : A Man's a Prodigy.

Dryd : Oedip :

That I could reach the Axle where the pins are
Which bolt this Frame ; that I might pull' em out,
And pluck all into Chaos with myself !
Who would not fall with all the World about him ?

[Ben] Johnson's Catil[ine's] Consp[iracy].

I thank the Gods, no secret Thoughts reproach me :
No, I dare challenge Heaven, to turn me outward,
And shake my soul quite empty in your Sight ;

Dryd : (1).

There is no Courage but in Innocence ;
No Constancy but in a honest Cause.

South[erne] Fate of Cap[ua].

(1) Underscored with pencil.

What stronger Breast-plate than a Heart untaint'd
Thrice is he arm'd that has his Quarrel just ;
And he but naked though lock'd up in Steel,
Whose Conscience with Injustice is corrupted.

Shak : Hen : VI.

'Tis not for Nothing that we Life pursue ;
It pays our Hopes with something still that's New ?
Each Day's a Mistress unenjoy'd before ;
Like Travellers, we're pleas'd with seeing more.

Dr. Auren [*Dryden : Aurenge-Zebe, act IV*].

How vainly would dull Moralists impose
Limits on Love, whose Nature brooks no Law ?
Love is a God, & like a God, should be
Inconstant, with unbounded Liberty ;
Rove as he list.

Otw[*ay*]. *D. Carlos.*

. . . . . What so hard, so stubborn, or so fierce,
But Music for the Time will change its Nature ?
The Man who has not Music in his soul,
Or is not touch'd with concord of sweet sounds,
If fit for Treasons, Stratagems, & spoils,
The Motions of his Mind are dull as Night,
And his Affections dark as Erebus :
Let no such Man be trusted.

Shak : Jew of Ven :

Music has charms to sooth a savage Breast,
To soften Rocks, or bend a knotted Oak.
I've read that Things inanimate have mov'd,
And, as with living souls, have been inform'd
By magic Numbers & persuasive sound.

Congr[*eve*]. *Mourn*[*ing*]. *Br*[*ide*].

Let there be Music, let the Master touch
The sprightly String, & softly breathing Lute.
Till Harmony rouse ev'ry gentle passion,
Teach the cold Maid to lose her Fears in Love,
And the fierce youth to languish at her Feet.
Begin : ev'n Age itself is chear'd with Music,
It wakes a glad Remembrance of our Youth,
Calls back joys, & warms us into Transport.

                    Rowe's F[air] Penit [ent].

We break no Laws either of Gods or Men :
So, if we fall, it is with Reputation ;
A Fate which Cowards shun, & brave Men seek.
If Cæsar punish Men for speaking Truth,
My honest Tongue shall dare his utmost Doom.

   [John Sheffield duke of] *Buck[inghamshire] : Jul[ius]*
        Cæs[ar] altered from Shak : Act : 1. Sc : 2.

I know where I shall wear this Dagger then :
Cassius from Bondage will deliver Cassius.
Herein the poor are rich, the Weak most strong
By this the wretched mock at base Oppression
The meanest are victorious o'er the mighty.
Not Tow'rs of Stone, Nor Walls of harden'd Brass,
Nor airless Dungeons, the poor Strength of Tyrants.
Not all their strongest Guards, nor heaviest Chains
Can in the least controul the mighty spirit.
For noble Life, when weary of itself,
Has allways Power to skake it off at pleasure
Since I know this, know all the World besides,
That part of Tyranny prepar'd for me,
I can & will defy.
                              And so can I.

Thus ev'ry Bondman in his own Hand bears
The Pow'r to cancel his Captivity.
And why should Cæsar be a Tyrant then
Poor Man ! I know he would not be a Wolf,

But that he sees the Romans are but Sheep :
He were no Lion if we were not Lambs.

Id : *Sc* : 5.

...Where does Nature or the Will of Heav'n
Subject a Creature to one like itself ?
Man is the only Brute enslaves his Kind.

Buck : *Death of Marc* : *Brut* : *Act.* 1. *Sc* : 3.

. . . . . If hearing Lyes
With greedy Ears, & soon beleiving them ;
If misinterpreting whate'er I do,
And representing Things in foulest Colours,
Can be call'd wronging, who was e'er so wrong'd ?

Id : *Act* : 4. *Sc.* : 3.

. . . . . Wed her !
No ! were she all Desire could wish, as fair
As would the vainest of her sex be thought,
With Wealth beyond what woman's pride could waste,
She should not cheat me of my Freedom.   Marry !
When I am old & weary of the World,
I may grow desperate,
And take a Wife to mortify withal.

Otways' Orph[*an*] *Act* : 1.

. . . . . Your sex
Was never in the Right ; Y'are all ways false,
Or silly ; ev'n your Dresses are not more
Fantastic than your Appetites ; you think
Of nothing twice : Opinion you have none.
To Day y'are nice, tomorrow not so free ;
Now smile, then frown ; now sorrowful, then glad
Now pleas'd now not ; And all you know not why ?
Virtue you affect, inconstancy's your practice ;
And when your loose Desires once get Dominion

No hungry churl feeds coarser at a Feast ;
Ev'ry rank Fool goes down.

Id :

Who'd be that sordid foolish Thing call'd Man,
To cringe thus, fawn, & flatter for a pleasure,
Which Beasts enjoy so very much above him ?
The lusty Bull ranges through all the Field,
And from the Herd singling his Female out,
Enjoys her, & abandons her at will.

Id :

No Flattery, Boy ! an honest Man can't live by't
It is a little sneaking art, which knaves
Use to cajole & soften Fools withal.
If thou hast Flattery in thy Nature, out with't,
Or send it to a Court, for there 'twill thrive.

Id : Act. 2.

. . . . . shun
The Man that's singular, his Mind's unsound
His spleen o'erweighs his Brains ; but above all,
Avoid the politic, the factious Fool,
The busy, buzzing, talking, harden's knave,
The quaint smooth-rough, that sins against his Reason,
Calls saucy loud suspicion, public Zeal,
And Mutiny, the Dictates of his Spirit ;
Be very careful how you make new Freinds.

Otw[ay] Orph[an]. Act : 3.

I'd leave the World for him that hates a Woman,
Woman the Fountain of all human Frailty !
What mighty Ills have not been done by Woman ?
Who was't betray'd the Capitol ?   A Woman.
Who lost Marc Anthony the World ? A Woman.
Who was the Cause of a long ten years War,

And laid at last old Troy in ashes ?   Woman.
Destructive, damnable, deceitful Woman !
Woman to Man first as a Blessing giv'n,
When Innocence & Love were in their Prime ;
Happy a while in Paradise they lay,
But quickly Woman long'd to go astray ;
Some foolish new Adventure needs must prove,
And the first Devil she saw, she chang'd her Love ;
To his Temptations lewdly she inclin'd
Her soul, & for an Aple damn'd Mankind.

Id :

.........All the Heav'n they hope for is Variety.
One lover to another still succeeds,
Another, & another after that,
And the last Fool is welcome as the former,
Till, having lov'd his Hour out, he gives place
And mingles with the Herd that goes before him.

Rowe's Fair Penit[ent] Act. 1.

You blast the Fair with Lies because they scorn you
Hate you like Age, like Ugliness & Impotence ;
Rather than make you bless'd they would die Virgins
And stop the propagation of Mankind.

Id : Act : 2.

Can there in Women be such glorious Faith ?
Sure all ill stories of thy Sex are false !
O Woman ! lovely Woman ! Nature made thee
To temper Man : we had been Brutes without you :
Angels are painted fair to look like you :
There's in you all that we beleive of Heav'n,
Amazing Brightness, purity & Truth,
Eternal joy, & everlasting Love.

Otw[ay] Ven[ice] preser[ved] Act. 1.

Cowards are scar'd with Threatnings ; Boys are whipt
Into Confessions : but a steady Mind
Acts of itself, ne'er asks the Body Counsel.
Give him the Tortures ! Name but such a Thing
Again, by Heav'n I'll shut these Lips for ever.
Not all your Racks, your Engines, or your Wheels
Shall force a Groan away, that you may guess at.

       Id : *Act.* : 4.

. . . . . You want to lead
My Reason blindfold, like a Hamper'd Lion,
Check'd of its nobler Vigour ; then when bated
Down to obedient Tameness, make it couch,
And shew strange tricks, which you call signs of Faith
So silly souls are gull'd, & you get Money.
Away ; no more.

       Id. : *Act.* 5.

Look round, how Providence bestows alike
Sunshine & Rain, to bless the fruitful year,
On different Nations, all of different Faiths ;
And (tho' by several Names & Titles worship'd))
Heav'n takes the various Tribute of their Praise ;
Since all agree to own, at least to mean,
One best, one greatest, only Lord of all.

    Rowe's Tamerl[*ane*]. *Act.* 3. *Sc*: 2.

. . . . . to subdue th'unconquerable Mind,
To make one Reason have the same Effect
Upon all Apprehensions ; to force this,   ·
Or this Man, just to think, as thou & I do ;
Impossible ! unless Souls were alike
In all, which differ now like human Faces.

       Ib :

Yet ere thou rashly urge my Rage too far,
I warn thee to take Heed ; I am a Man,

And have the Frailties common to Man's Nature ;
The fiery seeds of Wrath are in my Temper,
And may be blown up to so fierce a Blaze,
As Wisdom cannot rule. Know, thou hast touch'd me
Ev'n in the nicest, tenderest part, my Honour
My Honour !   which,like Pow'r, disdains being question'd ;

Id : Act. 4. Sc : 1.

Women, like summer storms, awhile are cloudy,
Burst out in Thunder, & impetuous Show'rs ;
But straight the Sun of Beauty dawns abroad,
And all the fair Horison is serene.

Id : Act. 5. Sc. 1.

. . . . . . Say now Melissa
Is there among the Daughters of Affliction
One so forlorn as poor Eurydice ?

Mallet's Euridice. Act. 1, Sc. 1.

Would Tears, my gracious Mistress, aught avail us
Methinks these aged Eyes could number Drops
With falling Clouds, or the perpetual Stream.

Ib : Sc. 4.

...By Heav'n my Soul can form
No Wish, no Thought but her. I tell thee, Medor
With Blushes tell thee, this proud Charmer reigns
Unbounded o'er my Reason. I have try'd
Each shape, each Art of varied Love to win' her ;
Alternate Prayers, & Threats, the soothing Skill
Of Passionate Sincerity, The Fire
Of rapturous Vows, but all these Arts were vain.
Her rooted Hate is not to be remov'd.
And 'twas my soul's first Aim, the towering Passion
Of all my Wishes, to prevail in this.

Id : Sc : 6.

What is the blooming Tincture of a skin,
To Peace of Mind, to Harmony within ?
What the bright sparkling of the finest Eye.
To the soft soothing of a calm reply ?
Can Comeliness of Form, or shape, or Air,
With comeliness of Words, or Deeds, compare ?
No ; — those at first th'unwary Heart may gain ;
But these, these only can that Heart retain.

The Art of charming.

. . . . . Whatsoever
Fortune decrees, still let us call to Mind
Our Freindship, & our Honour.   And since Love
Condemns us to Rivals for one Prize,
Let us contend as Freinds & brave Men ought,
With Openness & justice to each other ;
That he who wins the fair one to his Arms,
May take her as the Crown of great Desert :
And if the wretched Loser does repine,
His own Heart & the World may all condemn him.

Rowe's Jane Gray. Act. 1.

I had beheld, ev'n her whole sex, unmov'd,
Look'd o'er 'em like a Bed of gaudy Flowers,
That lift their painted Heads, & live a Day,
Then shed their trifling Glories unreguarded :
My Heart disdain'd their Beauties, till she came
With ev'ry Grace that Nature's Hand could give.

Id : Act. 3.

. . . . . Thy narrow soul
Knows not the God-like glory of forgiving :
Nor can thy cold, thy ruthless Heart conceive,
How large the Power, how fix'd the Empire is,
Which Benefits confer on generous Minds :
Goodness prevails upon the stubborn'st Foes,
And conquers more than ever Cæsar's sword did.

Id : Act. 5. Sc : 1.

And canst thou tell ? who gave thee to explore
The secret Purposes of Heav'n, or taught thee
To set a Bound to Mercy unconfin'd ?
But know, thou proud, perversely judging Winchester
Howe'er you hard imperious Censures doom,
And portion out our Lot in Worlds to come ;
Those who with Honest Hearts pursue the Right,
And follow faithfully Truth's sacred Light,
Tho' suffering here shall from their Sorrows cease,
Rest with the Saints, & dwell in endless Peace.

Ib : Act. 5. Sc. last.

Retiring from the popular noise, I seek
This unfrequented place to find some ease,
Ease to the Body some, none to the Mind
From restless Thoughts, that like a deadly swarm
Of Hornets arm'd, no sooner found alone
But rush upon me thronging, & present
Times past, what once I was, & what am now.

Milton's Samson Agonistes. v. 16.

But what is strength without a double share
Of Wisdom, vast, unweildy, burdensome,
Proudly secure, yet liable to fall
By weakest subtleties, not made to rule,
But to subserve where Wisdom bears Command.

Id : v. 53.

Suffices that to me Strength is my Bane,
And proves the Source of all my Miseries ;
So many, & so huge, that each apart
Would ask a Life to wail ;   .   .   .   .   .

Id : v. 63.

Scarce Haf I seem to live, dead more than half
O ! dark, dark, dark, amid the Blaze of Noon,

Irrecoverably dark, total eclipse
Without all Hopes of Day ! —

Id : *v.* 79

For him I reckon not in high estate
Whom long Descent of Birth
Or the Sphere of Fortune raises ;

Id : *v.* 170.

. . . . . apt Words have pow'r to suage
The Tumours of a troubled Mind,
And are as Balm to fester'd Wounds.

Id : *v.* 184.

. . . . . for I learn
Now of my own Experience, not by Talk,
How counterfeit a Coin they are who Freinds
Bear in their Superscription, (of the most
I would be understood) ; in prosp'rous Days
They swarm, but in adverse withdraw their Heads
Not to be found, though sought.

Id : *v.* 187.

. . . . . tell me, Freinds,
Am I not sung & proverb'd for a Fool
In ev'ry street ? do they not say, how well
Are come upon him his Deserts ?

Id : *v.* 203.

Deject not then so overmuch thyself,
Who hast of Sorrow thy full Load besides,

Id : *v.* 213.

. . . . . who think not God at all
If any be, they walk obscure ;
For of such Doctrine never was there school,
But the Heart of the Fool,
And no Man therein Doctor but himself.

Id : *v.* 295.

Nothing of all these Evils hath befall'n me
But justly ; I myself have brought them on ;
Sole Author, I, sole Cause ; if ought seem vile,
As vile hath been my Folly. . . . .

Id : v. 374.

. . . . . thou bear'st
Enough, & more, the Burden of that Fault
Bitterly hast thou paid, & still art paying
That rigid score. . . . .

Id : v. 430.

So much I feel my genial spirits droop,
My Hopes all flat, Nature within me seems
In all her Functions weary of herself,
My Race of Glory run, & Race of Shame,
And I shall shortly be with them that rest.

Id : v. 594.

. . . . . If Weakness may excuse,
What Murderer, what Traitor, Parricide,
Incestuous, sacrilegious, but may plead it ?
All Wickedness is Weakness : That plea therefore
With God or Man will gain thee no Remission.

Id : v. 831.

Nor think me so unwary or accurs'd,
To bring my Feet again into the Snare
Where once I have been caught.

Id : v. 930.

Fame, if not double-fac'd, is double-mouth'd,
And with contrary Blast proclaims most Deeds
On both his Wings, one black, the other white,
Bears greatest Names in his wild airy Flight.

Id : v. 971.

It is not Virtue, Wisdom, Valour, Wit,
Strength, Comeliness of shape, or amplest Merit
That Woman's Love can win or long inherit ;
But what it is, hard is to say,
Harder to hit,
(Which way soever Men refer it)
Much like thy Riddle Samson in one Day
Or sev'n, though one should musing sit.

Id : *v.* 1010.

Is it for that such outward Ornament
Was lavish'd on their Sex, that inward Gifts
Were left for Haste unfinished, judgment scant,
Capacity not rais'd to apprehend
Or value what is best
In Choice, but oftest to affect the Wrong ?
Or was too much of Self-Love mix'd,
Of Constancy no Root infix'd,
That either they love Nothing, or not long ?
Whate'er it be to wisest Men & best
Seeming at first all-heav'nly under Virgin Vail
Soft, modest, meek, demure,
Once join'd, the contrary she proves, a Thorn
Intestine, far within defensive arms
A cleaving Mischeif, in his play to Virtue
Adverse & turbulent, or by her Charms
Draws him away inslav'd
With Dotage, & his sense deprav'd
To Folly & shameful Deeds which Ruin ends.
What pilot so expert but needs must wreck,
Imbark'd with such a steersmate at the Helm ?
Favour'd of Heav'n who finds
One virtuous rarely found,
That in domestic good combines :
Happy that House ! his way to peace is smooth
But Virtue which breacks through all opposition

And all Temptations can remove,
Most shines, & most is acceptable above.
Therefore God's universal Law
Gave to Man despotic power
Over his Female in due awe,
Nor from that Right to part an Hour,
Smile she or lour :
So shall he least Confusion draw
On his whole Life, no sway'd
By female Usurpation, or dismay'd.

Id : v. 1025.

. . . . . Who but rather turns
To heav'n's broad fire his unconstrained view,
Than to the glimmering of a waxen flame ?
Who that, from Alpine heights his lab'ring eye
Shoots round the wide horizon to survey
The Nile or Ganges roll his wasteful tide
Thro' mountains, plains, thro' empires black with shade
And continents of sand ; will turn his gaze
To mark the windings of a scanty rill
That murmurs at his feet ?   the high born soul
Disdains to rest her heav'n aspiring wing
Beneath it's nature quarry.

[Mark Akenside] *Pleasures of Imagn. B.* i. *v.* 174.

Does beauty ever deign to dwell where health
And active use are strangers ? is her charm
Confess'd in ought, whose most peculiar ends
Are lame and fruitless ? or did nature mean
This awful stamp the herald of a lie ?
To hide the shame of discord and disease,
And catch with fair hypocrisy the heart
Of idle faith ?

Id. B. i. *v.* 350.

Oh ! blest of heaven, whom not the languid songs
Of luxury, the syren ! not the bribes
Of sordid wealth, nor all the gaudy spoils
Of pageant honor can seduce to leave
Those ever blooming sweets, which from the store
Of nature fair imagination culls
To charm th'inlivend'd soul ! What tho' not all
Of mortal offspring can attain the heights
Of envied life ; tho' only few possess
Patrician treasures or imperial state ;
Yet nature's care, to all her children just,
With richer treasures and an ampler state
Endows at large whatever happy man
Will deign to use them. . . . .
. . . . . Not a breeze
Flies o'er the meadow, not a cloud imbibes
The setting sun's effulgence, not a strain
From all the tenants of the warbling shade
Ascends, but whence his bosom can partake
Fresh pleasure unreprov'd nor thence partakes
Fresh pleasure only : for th'attentive mind,
By this harmonious action on her powr's
Becomes herself harmonious : wont so long
In outward things to meditate the charm
Of sacred order, soon she seeks at home
To find a kindred order, to exert
Within herself this elegance of love,
This fair inspired delight : her temper'd pow'rs
Refine at length, and every passion wears
A chaster, milder, more attractive mien.
But if to ampler prospects. . . . .
. . . . . the mind
Exalt her daring eye, then mightier far
Will be the change, and nobler.   Would the forms
Of senile custom cramp her gen'rous powr's ?
Would sordid policies, the barb'rous growth
Of ignorance and rapine bow her down
To tame pursuits, to indolence and fear ?

Lo ! she appeals to nature, to the winds
And rolling waves, the sun's unwearied course,
The elements and seasons : all declare
For what th'eternal maker has ordain'd
The pow'rs of man : we feel within ourselves
His energy divine : he tells the heart
He meant, he made us to behold and love
What he beholds and loves, the gen'ral orb
Of live and being ; to be great like him
Beneficent and active. Thus the men
Whom nature's works can charm, with God himself
Hold conserve ; grow familiar day by day,
With his conceptions ; act upon his plan ;
And form to his the relish of their souls.

Pl. of Imagn. B. 3. v. 568.

On my strain
Perhaps ev'n now some cold fastidious judge
Casts a disdainful eye ; and calls my toil,
And calls the love and beauty which I sing
The dream of folly. Thou grave censor ! say,
Is beauty then a dream, because the glooms
Of dulness hang too heavy on thy sense
To let her shine upon thee?

Id : v. 443.

Ut flos in septes secretis nascitur hortis
Ignotus pecori, nullo contusus aratro.
Quem mulcent aurae, firmat sol, educat embe,
Multi illum pueri, multae cupiere puellae.
Idem, cum tenui carptus deflaruit ungui,
Nulli illum pueri, nullae cupiere puellae.
Sic virgo, dum intacta manet, dum cara suis:
Cum castum amisit, polluto corpore, florem,
Nec pueris jucunda manet, nec cara puellis.

Yet shall thy grave with rising flow'rs be drest,
And the green turf lie lightly on thy breast:
There shall the morn her earliest tears bestow,
There the first roses of the year shall blow;
While Angels with their silver wings o'ershade
The ground now sacred by thy reliques made.
So peaceful rests without a stone, a name,
What once had beauty, titles wealth and fame.
How lov'd, how honour'd once, avails thee not,
To whom related, or by whom begot;
A heap of dust alone remains of thee,
'Tis all thou art, and all the proud shall be!
                              Pope. elegy. v. 63.

Adieu, ye vales, ye mountains, streams and groves,
Adieu ye shepherds' rural lays and loves;
Adieu, my flocks; farewell, ye sylvan crew;
Daphne, farewell; and all the world adieu!

Pope, Past. 4 v. 89

Beatus ille, qui procul negotiis
  Ut prisca gens mortalium
Paterna rura bobus exercet suis,
  Solutus omni foenore;
Forumque vitat, et superba civium
  Potentiorum limina.
Libet jacere modo sub antiqua ilice
  modo in tenaci gramine:
Labuntur altis interim rivis aquae;
  Queruntur in silvis aves;
Fontesque lymphis obstrepunt manantibus,
  Somnos quod invitet leves.
At cum tonantis annus hibernus Jovis
  Imbres nivesque comparat
Aut trudit acres hinc et hinc multa cane
  Apros in obstantes plagas;
Aut amite levi rara tendit .. retia,
  Turdis edacibus dolos;
Quod si pudica mulier in partem juvans
  Domum et dulces liberos,
Sacrum vetustis exstruat lignis focum
  Lassi sub adventum viri,

The fierce season of blazing dog-days cannot
touch thee ; thou provides a pleasant coolness
to the bullocks tired by the plough and to the
vagabonds flocks. Thou too wilt become one of
the famous fountains.

Oh swift as wheels that kindly roll,
Our life is hurrying to the goal ;
A scanty dust to feed the wind,
Is all the trace 't will leave behind

> *(Thomas Moore's translation)*

My soul to festive feelings true,
One pang of envy never knew ;
And little has it learn'd to dread
The gall that Envy's tongue can shed.

> *(Thomas Moores' translation)*

Te flagrantis atrox hora caniculæ
Nescit tangere ; tu frigus amabile
Fessis vomere tauris
Præbes, et pecori vago.
Fies nobilium tu quoque fontium.

Hor. Lib. 3, *ode* 13.

Τροχὸς ἄρματος γὰρ οἶα
Βίοτος τρέχει κυλισθείς.
Ὀλίγη δὲ κεισόμεσθα
Κόνις, ὀστέων λυθέντων.

Anac. Od. 4.

Φθόνον οὐκ οἶδ, ἐμὸν ἦτορ,
Φθόνον οὐ δείδια δυκτὴν
Φιλολοιδόροιο γλώττης
Φεύγω βέλεμνα κοῦφα

Anac. Od. 42.

. . . , . Now from the town
Buried in smoke; and sleep, and noisome damps,
Oft let me wander o'er the dewy fields
Where freshness breathes, and dash the trembling drops
From the bent bush, as thro the verdant maze
Of sweet-brier hedges I pursue my walk ;
Or taste the smell of daisy ; or ascend
Some eminence, . . . ;
And see the country far diffus'd around,
One boundless blush, one white-empurpled show'r
Of mingling blossoms ;   here the raptur'd eye
Hurries from joy to joy, and, hid beneath
The fair profusion, yellow Autumn skies.

Thompson's (sic) Spring. 101.

Let us, Amanda, timely wise,
Improve the hour that swiftly flies
And, in soft rapture, waste the day
Among the shades of Endermay.
For soon the winter of the year
And age, life's winter, will appear :
At this, thy living bloom must fade ;
As that will strip the verdant shade,
Our taste of pleasure then is o'er ;
The feather'd singsters love no more :
And when they droop and we decay.

Mallet's poems.

O scap'd from life !   O safe on that calm shore,
Where sin, and pain, and passion are no more !

Mallet's Poems.

In lonely walks and awful cells,
Secluded from the light and rain,
The cherub peace with virtue dwells
And solitude and silence reign.
The babbler's voice is heard not here
To heav'n the sacred pile belongs
Each wall returns the whisper'd pray'r,
And echoes but to holy songs.

Song by Moore.

[*From The Nun, a cantata*, in Edward Moore : *Poems and Plays*, 1756].

Hail midnight shades ! hail venerable dome !
By age more venerable ; sacred shore,
Beyond time's troubled sea, where never wave,
Where never wind of passion or of guilt
Or suffering or of sorrow, shall invade
The calm, sound night of those who rest below.
The weary are at peace : the small and great,
Life's voiage ended, meet and mingle here.
Here sleeps the prisoner safe, nor feels his chain,
Nor hears th'oppressor's voice. The poor and old,
With all the sons of mourning, fearless now
Of want or woe, find unalarm'd repose.
Proud greatness too, the tyranny of power,
The grace of beauty, and the force of youth,
And name and place, are here, for ever lost !

Mallet's Excursion.

Thyrsis — tis he ! the wisest and the best !
Lamented shade ! whom ev'ry gift of heav'n
Profusely blest : all learning was his own.
Pleasing his speech, by nature taught to flow,
Persuasive sense and strong, sincere and clear.
His manners greatly plain ; a noble grace
Self-taught, beyond the reach of mimic art,
Adorn'd him : his calm temper winning mild ;

Nor Pity softer, nor was truth more bright.
Constant in doing well, he neither sought
Nor shun'd applause. No bashful merit sigh'd
Near him neglected : sympathizing he
Wip'd off the tear from Sorrows' clouded eye
With kindly hand, and taught her heart to smile.

Mallet's Excursion.

. . . , . a place of tombs
Waste, desolate, where Ruin dreary dwells,
Broodings o'er sightless sculls and crumbling bones.
Ghastful he sits, and eyes with stedfast glare
                                 the falling roof,
The time-shook arch, the column grey with moss,
The leaning wall, the sculptur'd stone defac'd.

Mallet's Excursion.

I have turn'd o'er the catalogue of woes,
Which sting the heart of man, and find none equal;
It is the Hydra of calamities ;
The seven fold death : the jealous are the damn'd.
O jealousy, each other passion's calm
To thee, thou conflagration of the soul !
Thou king of torment ! thou grand counterpoise
For all the transports beauty can inspire !

Young's Revenge. Act.2.

What is the world ? — thy school, O misery !
Our only lesson is to learn to suffer ;
And he who knows not that, was born for nothing.
Tho' deep my pange, and heavy at my heart,
My comfort is, each moment rakes away
A grain at least from the dead load that's on me
And gives a nearer prospect of the grave.
But put it most severely — should I live —

Live long — alas ! there is no length in time ;
Not in thy time, O man ! what's fourscore years ?
Nay, what indeed the age of time itself
Since cut from out eternity's wide round ?

Young's Revenge. Act. 2.

This hand is mine. O what a hand is here !
So soft, souls sink into it, and are lost.

Young's Revenge. Act. 4.

Why did I 'leave my tender father's wing,
And venture into love ? that maid that loves,
Goes out to sea upon a shatter'd plank.
And puts her trust in miracles for safety.

. . . .

This vast and solid earth, that blazing sun,
Those skies thro' which it rolls, must all have end.
What then is man ? the smallest part of nothing.
Day buries day ; month, month ; and year the year :
Our life is but a chain of many death.
Can then death's self be fear'd ? our life much rather
Life is the desart, life the solitude ;
Death joins us to the great majority ;
Tis to be born to Platos and to Cæsars ;
Tis to be great for ever ;
Tis pleasure, tis ambition, then, to die.

Id. Ib.

I am no gewgaw for the throng to gaze at :
Some are design'd by nature for shew ;
The tinsel and the feather of mankind.

Young's Brothers. Act. 1.

We run our fates together ; you deserve
And she can judge ; proceed we then like friends,
And he who gains the heart, and gains it fairly
Let him enjoy his gen'rous rival's too.

Id. Ib.

The days of life are sisters ; all alike ;
None just the same ; which serves to fool us on
Thro' blasted hopes, with change of fallacy ;
While joy is, like tomorrow, still to come ;
Nor ends the fruitless chace but in the grave.

Id.Ib.

Thrice happy they, who sleep in humble life,
Beneath the storm ambition blows, 'tis meet
The great should have the fame of happiness,
The consolation of a little envy ;
Tis all their pay for those superior cares,
Those pangs of heart their vassals ne'er can feel.

Id. Ib.

How vain all outward effort to supply
The soul with joy !   the noontide sun is dark,
And music discord, when the heart is low.

Id. Act.2.

Fate !   drop the curtain ; I can lose no more !

Young's Night Thoughts.

JEPHTHES

Oh happy security of a modest condition.He is happy indeed
who far from disturbances spend his years unknown in a
secure obscurity.

SYMMACHUS

But I would rather consider him happy whose virtue has
begotten an eternal honor, whom taken from the obscurity
of the ordinary people and freed of vulgar indolency
a well deserved glory consecrates in centuries to come.
But the man who gives himself up to slumbering a worthless
existence and spends an inert life like an animal, there
is not difference in my opinion whether he is dead or
lives a life more obscure than death, since in both cases
he is buried under the same oblivion.

.   .   .   .

Honor, victory, marvelous words to tell, as well as distinction, triumph and glory acquired in war. But these
things which in appearance are so sweet, if you examine
them more exactly conceal in themselves the bitterness
of gall. Has ever good fortune shone so constantly for any
man that bad fortune has not compensated it on an even
scale. The cruel changes of fate temper unhappiness with
happy things and happiness with sadness.

Fate has always mingled sadness to joy and this fate forsooth
is to be considered the best of all when only few sad things
are hidden under many happy ones.

Jepthes (sic). O grata sortis infimæ securitas.
Felice natum videre illum existimo,
Procul tumultu qui remotus exigit
Ignotum ævum tuta per silentia.

Symmachus. At ego beatum potius illum duxero,
Cui vera virtus peperit æternum decus.
Quem de tenebris erutum popularibus
Splendore, vulgo et separatum a deside
Gloria futuris merita sæclis consecrat.
At qui sopori deditus et ignaviæ est,
Et vitam inertem pecudis instar transigit,
Nil interesse opinor, an sit mortuus
An morte vitam obscuriorem duxerit,
Quum par utrumque supprimat silentium.

. . . .

Jephthes. Præclara dictu res honor, victoria.
Decus, triumphus, parta bello gloria.
At quæ videntur fronte prima suavia,
Eadem intuere proprius, et intelliges
Condita fellis acri amaritudine.
Fortuna nulli sic refulsit prospera ?
Adversa ut illam lance non penset pari :
Tristia secundis, et secunda tristibus
Vicessitudo acerba sortis temperat.

Buchanani Jephthes.

Acerba laetis sors utrinque miscuit :
Sed illa certe existimanda est optima
Quœ multa paucis læta condit tristibus.

Id. Ib.

Alas, sudden change of fortune. How in the interrupted series of events absolutely nothing pleasant has been left to the mortals.

Advice brings remedy to things which are in doubt. But he who seeks advice when there is no possibility of help, adds only stupidity to his misery.

To act foolishly on good authority is hardly to be sensible.

Such is the fortune of our life that unhappy things succeed happy ones as darkness follows daylight and rough weather the pleasant spring. There is no pure pleasure that pains do not spoil with their bitter gall the perfid inconstancy of fortune introduces terrible turns in the lives of men.

Fortune fears the courageous ; she crushes the coward.

He who gave a decision without hearing the second party, even if he decided justly, has not been just.

As a flower in the enclosure of a garden grows well protected against the flocks and untouched by the ploughshare, and is caressed by the breezes, made vigourous by the soil and taller by the rain, coveted by many young boys and many young girls, thus is a virgin as long as she remains pure and cherished by her family. But when her sullied body has lost the flower of its chastity, she no longer attracts the young men nor is she cherished by the young girls.

Heu mutatio subitæ sortis !
Ut perpetua serie lætum
Nil mortalibus usque relictum est !

Id. Ib.

Consilia dubiis remedium rebus ferunt.
Qui consulit, quum nullus auxilio est locus,
Addit miseriis sponte stultitiam suis.

Id. Ib.

Auctore magno desipere, pene sapere est.

Id. Ib.

Hœc minimum est addita nostræ
Vitæ sors, ut tristia lætis
Vicibus subeant, tenebræ ut soli,
Ut veri aspera bruma tepenti.
Nulla est adeo pura voluptas,
Quam non tetro felle dolores
Vitient : levitas perfida sortis
Vice sæva res hominum miscet.

Id. Ib.

Fortuna fortes metuit ; ignavos premit.

Senecæ Medea. 159.

Qui statuit aliquid parte inaudita altera,
Æquum licet statuerit, haud æquus fuit.

Id. Ib. 199.

Ut flos in septis secretis nascitur hortis
Ignotus pecori, nullo contusus aratro,
Quem mulcent auræ, firmat sol, educat imber,
Multi illum pueri, multæ cupiere puellæ.
Sic VIRGO, dum intacta manet, dum cara suis :
Cum castum amisit, polluto corpore, florem,
Nec pueris jucunda manet, nec cara puellis.

[Catullus LXII].

Happy the man who, free from business worries, like the men of the old days, tills with his oxen his ancestral fields without being harassed by mortgages... he keeps away from the Forum and the proud threshold of the powers that be... He likes to recline now under an ancient oak now on the thick grass. Meanwhile the brooks flow between their high banks ; birds warble in the woods and springs bubble with running water, a sweet invitation

Yet shall thy grave with rising flow'rs be drest,
And the green turf lie lightly on thy breast.
There shall the morn her earliest tears bestow,
There the first roses of the year shall blow ;
While Angels with their silver wings o'ershade
The ground now sacred by thy reliques made.
So peaceful rests without a stone, a name,
What once had beauty, titles, wealth and fame.
How lov'd, how honour'd once, avails thee not,
To whom related, or by whom begot ;
A heap of dust alone remains of thee,
Tis all thou art, and all the proud shall be !

Pope. elegy. v. 63.

Adieu, ye vales, ye mountains, streams and graves.
Adieu, ye shepherds' rural lays and loves ;
Adieu, my flocks ; farewell, ye sylvan crew ;
Daphne, farewell ; and all the world adieu.

Pope. Past. 4. *v.* 89.

Beatus ille, qui procul negotiis
Ut prisca gens mortalium,
Paterna rura bobus exercet suis,
Solutus omni fænore :

.   .   .   .   -

Forumque vitat, et superba civium
Potentiorum limina.

.   .   .   .   -

Libet jacere modo sub antiqua ilice
Modo in tenaci gramine :
Labuntur altis interim rivis aquæ ;
Quæruntur in silvis aves ;
Fontesque lymphis obstrepunt manantibus,

to repose. But when the wintry season of thundering
Jove brings back rains and snows, either with his pack
of hounds he drives the fierce boars into the traps, or
arranges large meshed nets on polished sticks to snare
the greedy thrushes ; ... If a modest wife who does
her part in tending the house and her dear children,
piles high the sacred hearth with dry firewood waiting
for the return of her tired husband, gathers in a pen
made of wattles the fat ewes in order to milk their
distended udders, and drawing from the keg new sweet
wine prepares a meal which she had not to pay for...
Amid such feasts what joy to see the sheep hurrying
back to the farm after pasturing, to see the tired
oxen dragging along the upturned ploughshare and
the young slaves, industrious swarm of an opulent house,
seated around the resplendent Lares.

Somnos quod invitet leves.
At cum tonantis annus hibernus Jovis
Imbres nivesque comparat
Aut trudit acres hinc et hinc multa cane
Apres in obstantes plagas ;
Aut amite levi rara tendit retia,
Turdis edacibus dolos ;

. . . .

Quod si pudica mulier in partem juvans
Domum et dulces liberos,
Sacrum vetustis exstruat lignis focum
Lassi sub adventum viri,
Claudensque textis cratibus lætum pecus,
Distenta siccet ubera ;
Et horna dulci vina promens dolio,
Dapes inemptas apparet.

. . . .

Has inter epulas, ut juvat pastas oves
Videre properantes domum.
Videre fessos vomerem inversum boves
Collo trahentes languidos ;
Positosque vernas, ditis examen domus,
Circum renidentes Lares.

                              Hor. epod. 2.

An unfrequented vale, o'ergrown with trees,
Mossy and old, within whose lonesome shade
Ravens and birds ill omen'd only dwell.
No sound to break the silence, but a brook,
That bubbling, winds among the weeds : no mark
Of any human shape had been there,
Unless a skeleton of some poor wretch,
Who had long since, like me by love undone
Sought that sad place out, to despair and die in.

Rowe's Fair penitent. [act II, sc. I. v. 20].

Be juster heaven ; such virtue punish'd thus,
Will make us think Chance rules all above,
And shuffles with a random hand, the lots
Which man is forc'd to draw...

The cheif like a whale of ocean, whom all his
billows follow, poured his valor forth as a stream,
rolling his might along the shore.

Fingal. B. 1.

As two dark streams from high rocks meet, and
mix and roar on the plain, loud rough, and
dark in battle Melochlin and Innis fail : chief
mixed his stroke with chief, and man with man ;
steel clanging sounded or steel helmets are
cleft on high ; blood bursts and smokes around.
Strings murmur on the polished yews, darts
rush along the sky, spears fall like the circles
of light that gild the stormy face of the night.
As the troubled noise of the ocean when roll
the waves on high ; as the last peal of the
thunder of heaven, such is the noise of the
battle. tho' Cormac's hundred bards were there
to give the war to song ; feeble were the voices
of an hundred bards to send the deaths
future times. for many were the falls of the
heroes, and wide poured the blood of the valiant (1).

Fingal B. 1.

(1) The editions I was able to consult slightly differ from this version :
they read *feeble was the voice,* and *brave* instead of valiant.

As when winter torrents gushing from their great springs
in the mountains
towards a pass mix their fierce waters in a deep gorge, and
                                                                [far
off in the mountains the shepherd hears their thunder ;
in the same way shouting and dread arose from those
who had joined in battle.

They dashed together shields and spears, and the wild fury
of warriors protected with bronze breast plates, and the
bossed bucklers clashed against one another, and a great
din arose.

Making a bristling fence with spear opposed to spear ;
serried shield propped against shield, buckler against buckler
                                                                [and
helmet against helmet, and man against man.

They stand foot to foot and man to man.

Now shield is opposed to shield and buckler to buckler
and sword to sword, foot to foot and helmet to helmet.

HOMER   191

Ὡς δ᾽ὅτε χείμαρροι ποταμοί, κατ᾽ ὅρεσφι ῥέοντες
Ἐς μισγάγκειαν συμβαλλετον ὄβριμον ὕδωρ,
Κρουνῶν ἐκ μεγάλων, κοίλης ἔντοσθε χαράδρης,
Τῶν δέ τε τηλόσε δοῦπον ἐν οὔρεσι ἔκλυε ποιμήν ·
Ὡς τῶν μισγομένων γένετο ἰαχή τε φόβος τε.

Iliad. 4. 452.

Σὺν ῥ᾽ ἔβαλον ῥινούς, σὺν δ᾽ ἔγχεα, καὶ μένε᾽ ἀνδρῶν
Χαλκεοθωρήκων · ἀτὰρ ἀσπίδες ὀμφαλόεσσαι
Ἔπληντ᾽ ἀλλήλῃσι · πολὺς δ᾽ ὀρυμαγδὸς ὀρώρει.

Iliad. 4. v. 447.

Φράξαντες δόρυ δουρί, σάκος σάκει προθελύμνῳ ·
Ἀσπὶς ἄρ᾽ ἀσπίδ᾽ ἔρειδε, κόρυς κόρυν, ἀνέρα δ᾽ἀνήρ.

Iliad [13 v. 130].

.....hæret pedes pes, densusque viro vir.

Æ. 9. 361.

Jam clypeus clypeis, umbone repellitur umbo,
Ense minax ensis, pede pes, et cuspide cuspis.

Statius.

As roll a thousand waves to the rocks, so Swaran's host
[came on : as
meets a rock a thousand waves, so Inis-fail met Swaran.
Fingal. B. 1.

He had seen her like a beam of light that meets the sons
[of the cave
When they revisit the feilds of the sun, and bend their
[aching eyes.
Fingal.

The vanquished, if brave, are renowned ; they are like the
sun on a cloud when he hides his face in the south, but
looks again on the hills of grass.
Fingal. B. 6.

Oh that I could forget my friends till my footsteps cease
to be een ! till I come among them with joy ! and lay my aged
limbs in the narrow house !

Ossian's Conlath and Cuthona.

The dark and narrow house. — the maid of the tearful
eye. The son of songs, Carril of other times. — Grudar the
youth of her secret soul — he was the stolen sigh of her
soul. — said Connal's voice of wisdom. — Said the mouth
of the song. — The chief of the little soul. — The ages of
old, and the days of other years.
Ossian. passim.

Raise the song of mourning, O bards, over the land of
[strangers
They have but fallen before us : for one day we must fall.why
dost thou build the hall, son of the winged days ? thou loo-
[kest
from thy towers to day ; yet a few years and the blast of the
desert comes ; it howls in thy empty court, and whistles
[round

the half-worn sheild. and let the blast of the desert come!
We shall be renowned in our day. the mark of my arm shall
be in the battle, and my name in the song of bards ; raise
the song ; send round the shell ; and let joy be heard in
my hall. when thou, Sun of heaven, shalt fail ! if thou shall
fail, thou might light ! if thy brightness is for a season, like
Fingal, our fame shall survive thy beams. such was the song
of Fingal, in the day of his joy.

Ossian's Carthon.

O thou that rollest above, round as the sheild of my father,
Whence are thy beams, O sun ! thy everlasting light ? Thou
comest forth in their awful beauty and the stars hide themselves in the sky ; the moon, cold and pale, sinks in the
western wave. But thou thyself movest alone : who can be
companion of thy course! The oaks of the mountains fall: the
mountains themselves decay with years ; the ocean shrinks
and grows again : the moon herself is lost in heaven ; but
thou ! art for ever the same ; rejoicing in the brightness
of thy course. when the world is dark with tempests ; when
thunder rolls, and lightning flies ; thou lookest in the
beauty from the clouds, and laughest at the storm, but to
Ossian thou lookest in vain ; for he beholds thy beams no
more ; whither thy yellow hair flows on the eastern clouds,
or thou tremblest at the gates of the west. but thou art
perhaps like me, for a season, and thy years will have an
end. Thou shalt sleep in thy clouds, careless of the voice
of the morning. Exult then O sun! in the strength of thy
youth ! age is dark and unlovely ; it is like the glimmering
light of the moon, when it shines thro' broken clouds, and
the mist is on the hills ; the blast of North is on the plain ;
the traveller shrinks in the midst of his journey.

Ossian's [Carthon].

To stand and bear patiently the ways of the people
with whom you are, to sacrifice your tastes to them,
to accept with docility their fancies, not to oppose
anyone, never to put oneself before anybody, in such a
way it is very easy to acquire praise without arousing
jealousy and to make friends.

Sosia. Yes he arranged his life wisely, for in our days
      subservience engenders friendship, but truth en-
      genders hatred.

The human mind always inclines from toil to pleasure.

Facile omnes perferre ac pati,
Cum quibus erat cumque una, iis sese dedere ;
Eorum obsequi studiis ; adversus nemini ;
Numquam praeponens se illis, ita facillume
Sine invidia laudem invenias, et amicos pares.

So[*sia*] Sapienter vitam instituit ; namque hoc tempore,
Obsequium amicos, veritas odium parit.

Terent. Andr. act. 1, *sc.* 1, 35. [63].

. . . . . ingenium est omnium
Hominum ab labore proclive ad libidinem.

Id. v. 50. [78].

O ciel ! que tes rigueurs seroient peu redoutables,
Si la foudre d'abord accabloit les coupables !
Et que tes chatimens paroissent infinis,
Quand tu laisses la vie à ceux que tu punis.

Racine. Freres ennemis, act I, *sc.* 2.

Les autres ennemis n'ont que de courtes haines,
Mais quand de la nature on a brisé les chaînes,
Cher Attale, il n'est rien qui puisse reunir
Ceux que des nœuds si forts n'ont pas su retenir.
L'on hait avec exces lors que l'on hait un frere.

Ib. act 3, *v.* 6.

L'amour eut peu de part a cet hymen honteux
Et la seule fureur en alluma les feux.

Ib. act. I, *sc.* 3.

Son courage sensible a vos justes douleurs
Ne veut point de lauriers arrosez de vos pleurs.

Ib. Alexandre, act. 2., *sc.* I.

LANGHORNE

Sun of the soul whose chearful ray
  Darts o'er this gloom of life a smile ;
Sweet Hope, yet further gild my way,
  Yet light my weary steps awhile,
Till thy fair lamp dissolve in endless day.
O come ! & to my pensive eye
Thy far foreseeing tube apply,
Whose kind deception steals us o'er
The gloomy waste that lies before ;
Still opening to the distant sight
The sunshine of the mountain's height ;
Where scenes of fairer aspect rise
Elysian graves & azure skies.
  Life's ocean slept — the liquid gale
Gently mov'd the waving sail.
Fallacious Hope ! with flattering eye
You smiled to see the streamers fly.
The thunder bursts, the mad wind raves
From slumber wake the 'frighted waves :
You saw me, fled me thus distrest,
And tore your anchor from my breast.
  Yet come, fair fugitive again !
I love thee still, though false & vain.
Forgive me gentle Hope and tell
Where, far from me, you deign to dwell.
To soothe ambition's wild desires ;
To feed the lover's eager fires ;

To swell the Miser's mouldy store ;
To gild the dreaming chymist's ore ;
Are these thy cares ? or more humane
To loose the captive's war-worne chain,
And bring before his languid sight
The charms of liberty & light ;
The tears of drooping grief to dry ;
And hold thy glass to Sorrow's eye ?
Or dost thou more delight to dwell
With silence in the hermit's cell ?
To teach devotion's flame to rise,
And wing her vespers to the skies ;
To urge, with still returning care,
The holy violence of prayer ;
In rapt'rous visions to display
The realms of everlasting day,
And snatch from time the golden key,
That opens all eternity ?

Perchance on some unpeopled strand,
Whose rocks the raging tide withstand,
Thy soothing smile in desarts drear,
A lonely mariner may chear,
Who bravely holds his feeble breath,
Attack'd by famine, pain, & death.
With thee he bears each tedious day
Along the dreary beach to stray :
Whence their wild way his toil'd eyes strain
O'er the bosom of the main ;
And meet where distant surges rave,
A white sail in each foaming wave.
Doom'd from each native joy to part,
Each dear connection of the heart,
You the poor exile's steps attend,
The only undeserting friend.
You wing the slow-declining year ;
You dry the solitary tear ;
And oft, with pious guile, restore
Those scenes he must behold no more.

Vain Hope, thou harbinger of woe.
Ah no ! — that thought distracts my heart :
Indulge me, Hope, we must not part.
Direct the future as you please ;
But give me, give me present ease.

Langhorne's Hymn to Hope. Stanz. 1. 3. 6. 7. 8. 9. 10. 11. (1).

(1) This corresponds to stanzas 7, 8, 9, 10, 14, in John Langhorne : *Poetical works*. London 1804, 2 vols. In that edition line 6 of page 198 reads « war worn captive's chain ».

And Diomedes good at the war-cry slew Axylos, son of Teuthran who dwelt in well built Aristea, a man rich in properties and beloved by all men ; for he dwelt in a house by the road and gave pleasure to all.

Even as are the generations of leaves such are also those of men. As for the leaves, the wind scatters some upon the earth, but the forest when it bourgeons produces others when the season of spring comes.   In the same way a generation of men springs up when another passes away.

Ἄξυλον δ᾿ ἄρ ἔπεφνε, βοὴν ἀγαθὸς Διομήδης,
Τευθρανίδην, ὃς ἔναιεν εὐκτιμένη ἐν Ἀρισβῃ
Ἀφνειὸς βιότοιο, φίλος δ᾿ ἔεν ἀνθρώποισι ·
Πάντας γὰρ φιλέεσκεν, ὁδῷ ἔπι οἰκία νάων.

Il. ζ. 12,

Ὄιη περ φύλλων γενεή, τοίηδε, καὶ ἀνδρῶν ·
Φύλλα τὰ μέν τ᾿ ἄνεμος χαμάδις χέει, ἄλλα δ᾿ ὕλη
Τηλεθόωσα φύει, ἔαρος δ᾿ ἐπιγίγνεταὶ ὥρη ·
Ὡς ἀνδρῶν γενεή . ἡ μὲν φύει, ἡ δ᾿ ἀπολήγει.

Il. ζ. 14.6

[The following is a newspaper clipping pasted in book].

ELEGY

Sigh not ye winds, as passing o'er,
  The chambers of the dead ye fly !
Weep not, ye dew, for these no more
  Shall ever weep, shall ever sigh !

Why mourn ? the throbbing heart's at rest,
How still it lies within the breast !
Why mourn ? since death presents us peace,
And in the grave our sorrows cease.

The shatter'd bark, from adverse winds,
Rest in this peaceful haven finds,
And when the storms of life are past
Hope drops her anchor here at last.

Daughter of heaven, fair art thou ! the silence of thy
face is pleasant ! thou comest forth in loveliness : the
stars attend thy blue steps in the east. the clouds rejoice
in thy presence O moon, and brighten their dark brown
sides. who is like thee in heaven, daughter of the night,
the stars are ashamed in thy presence, and turn aside their
green sparkling eyes. Whither dost thou retire from thy
course, when the darkness of thy countenance grows ?
hast thou thy hall like Ossian ? dwellest thou in the shadow
of grief ? have thy sisters fallen from heaven ? are they
who rejoiced with thee, at night, no more ? Yes they have
fallen, fair light ! and thou dost often retire to mourn,
but thou thyself shalt fail one night ; and leave thy blue

path in heaven. the stars will then lift their green heads :
they. they who were ashamed in thy presence will rejoice.
Thou art now clothed with thy brightness : look from thy
gates in the sky. burst the cloud, O wind, that the daugnter
of night may look forth that the shaggy mountains may
brighten, and the ocean roll its blue waves in light.

Ossian's Darthula.

Where have ye been, ye Southern winds ! when the sons
of my love were deceived ? but ye have been sporting on
plains, and pursuing the thistle's beard. O that ye had been
rustling in the sails of Nathos, till the hills of Etha rose !
till they rose in their clouds, and saw their coming cheif !
long hast thou been absent, Nathos ! and the day of thy
return is past.

Ossian's Darthulah.

How long shall we weep on Lena ; or pour our tears in
Ullin ? the mighty will not return. Oscar shall not rise in
his strength, the valiant must fall one day, and be no more
known on his hills. where are our fathers, O warriors ! the
cheifs of the time of old ? they have set like stars that
have shone, we only hear the sound of their praise. but
they were renowned in their day, and the terror of other
times : thus shall we pass O warriors, in the day of our fall.
then let us be renowned when we may ; and leave our fame
behind us, like the last beams of the sun, when he hides his
red head in the west.

Ossian's Temora.

Dost thou force me from my place, replied the hollow
voice the people bend before me. I turn the battle in the
feild of the valiant. I look on the nations and they vanish :
my nostrils pour the blast of death. I come abroad on the
winds : the tempests are before my face ! but my dwelling is
calm, above the clouds. the feilds of my rest are pleasant.
he lifted high his shade spear ; and bent forward his terrible

height. but the king, advancing, drew his sword ; the blade
of dark-brown Luno. the gleaming part of the steel winds
thro' the gloomy ghost the form fell shapeless into air, like a
column of smoke, which the staff of the boy disturbs, as it
rises from the half-extinguished furnace. the spirit of Loda
shrieked as, rolled into himself he rose on the wind. Inistore
shook at the sound. the waves heard it on the deep : they
stopped in their course with fear.

Ossian's Carric-thura.

Nor slept the sword by thy side, thou last of Fingal's
race. Ossian rushed forward in his strength, and the people
fell before him ; as the grass by the staff of the boy; when
he whistles along the feild, and the grey beard of the thistle
falls. but careless the youth moves on ; his steps are towards
the desart.

Ossian's Lathmon.

THE BEGGAR

.   .   .   .   .   *inopemque paterni*
Et laris et fundi — Hor.
Pity the sorrows of a poor old man !
Whose trembling limbs have borne him to your door ;
Whose days are dwindled to the shortest span,
Oh ! give relief — and heav'n will bless your store.
  These tatter'd clothes my poverty bespeak,
These hoary locks proclaim my lengthen'd years,
And many a furrow in my grief-worn cheek
Has been the channel to a stream of tears.
  Yon house erected on the rising ground,
With tempting aspect drew me from my road,
For plenty there a residence has found,
And grandeur a magnificent abode.
  (Hard is the fate of the infirm & poor !)
Here craving for a morsel of their bread,
A pamper'd menial forced me from the door,

To seek a shelter in an humbler shed.

Oh ! take me to your hospitable dome,
Keen blows the wind, & piercing is the cold !
Short is my passage to the friendly tomb,
For I am poor, and miserably old.

Should I reveal the source of ev'ry grief,
If soft humanity e'er touch'd your breast,
Your hand would not withold the kind relief,
And tears of pity could not be represt.

Heav'n sends misfortunes — why should we repine ?
'Tis heav'n has brought me to the state you see :
And your condition may be soon like mine,
The child of sorrow, & of misery.

A little farm was my paternal lot,
Then like the lark, I sprightly hail'd the morn ;
But ah oppression forc'd me from my cot,
My cattle died, and blighted was my corn.

My daughter, once the comfort of my age !
Lur'd by a villain from her native home
Is cast, abandon'd, on the world's wide stage,
And doom'd in scanty poverty to roam (1).

[*Thomas Moss*].

[*Here 2/3ds of the page are cut away*].

On verso :

Sweet are the jasmine's breathing flowers
Sweet the soft falling vernal showers
Sweet is the gloom the grove affords
And sweet the notes of warbling birds.
But not the grove, nor rain, nor flowers
Nor all the feathered songsters' powers
Can ever sweet & pleasing be
Oh lovely FREEDOM, without thee.

(1) Quoted again in *Thoughts on English Prosody. M. E.* XVIII, 427.

While we are seeking life we are losing it, and without realising any of our wishes, we always act as if we were going to live and never do live.

As for me I do not worry about the hereafter, even if now the doom of death stands at my feet, for we are men and cannot live forever. To all of us death must happen.

. . . . . Dum quærimus, ævum
Perdimus, et nullo votorum fine beati,
Victuros agimus semper, nec vivimus unquam.

Manilius (1).

αὐτὰρ ἔγωγε
Ὕστερον οὐκ ἀλέγω, εἰ καὶ παρὰ ποσσὶν ὄλεθρος
Σήμερον ἡμετέροισι πέλει λυγρός οὔ τι γάρ ἄνδρες
Ζώομεν ἤματα πάντα · πότμος δ᾽ἐπὶ πᾶσι τέτυκται.

Q. [Smyrnaeus] Calaber. 6, 431.

(1) These two quotations were certainly added at a late date, as showed
by the handwriting and the color of the ink.

INDEX